Decision Analysis, Game Theory, and Information

Louis Kaplow
*Finn M. W. Caspersen and Household
International Professor of
Law and Economics
Harvard University*

Steven Shavell
*Samuel R. Rosenthal Professor of
Law and Economics
Director, John M. Olin Center for Law,
Economics, and Business
Harvard University*

Reprinted from
Analytical Methods for Lawyers

© 2004 By FOUNDATION PRESS
    395 Hudson Street
    New York, NY 10014
    Phone Toll Free 1–877–888–1330
    Fax (212) 367–6799
    fdpress.com
Printed in the United States of America

ISBN 1–58778–807–1

 TEXT IS PRINTED ON 10% POST CONSUMER RECYCLED PAPER

Preface

Lawyers frequently make strategic decisions regarding their clients' interests, ranging from whether to settle a lawsuit to what sort of contract design to propose. *Decision Analysis, Game Theory, and Information* teaches the basics of decision analysis and game theory, which are the fundamental tools used over the past half-century by clients, whether businesses, government institutions, other entities, or individuals. Special attention is given to the use of these techniques in litigation. An overview of moral hazard, adverse selection, and other problems of imperfect information, as well as an introduction to bargaining (negotiation), is also included. This Handbook can be used as a supplementary text for a first-year civil procedure course, and would also be appropriate for courses on negotiation, legal methods, or law and economics.

This Handbook is drawn from Foundation Press's textbook, *Analytical Methods for Lawyers*, which was created to accompany a course we and other professors have taught for the past five years at Harvard Law School. The course and the original text grew out of our joint realization that the traditional law school curriculum, with its focus on the development of analogical reasoning skills and legal writing and research, left many law students inadequately prepared for upper-level law courses and, more importantly, for legal practice in the modern world. Lawyers, whether corporate counsel or public interest advocates, must work in settings where effective argumentation and the giving of sound legal advice often depend on mastery of language and techniques derived from a range of disciplines that are staples of the modern business school curriculum but notably absent, in introductory form, from law school classrooms.

True, a number of students arrive at law school well equipped with general knowledge of some of these areas from their undergraduate or work experiences. Equally true, however, is that many, perhaps the majority, of law students are woefully underprepared in these areas. They may self-select away from upper-level courses in which their inadequate preparation would severely disadvantage them. These students will graduate from law school without a set of basic skills, the absence of which will hamper their development in almost any of the careers that law graduates now pursue. Moreover, even those students who do have strong general preparation are often unacquainted with how what they have learned may be used effectively by practicing lawyers. It has been our experience that many students are themselves acutely aware of their deficiencies (or are made aware of it when they encounter certain discussions in first-year classrooms or when they receive their first assignments in a summer job or internship). Such students are eager to have their legal education enhanced by material like that in this Handbook, which promises to demystify analytical concepts and quantitative techniques that they see as clearly relevant to success in their law school coursework and, ultimately, to success in their chosen careers. It is primarily for these students that this Handbook has been written.

Unlike traditional introductory treatments, this Handbook is not a dry or technical text, far removed from the world of law. Quite the opposite. Virtually every concept is introduced, explained, and applied in legal contexts. Additionally, this Handbook is designed to be used to facilitate problem-based classroom discussion, materials for which are available to instructors in a Teachers' Manual. The translation from theory to practice is not left for students to develop on their own, after graduation. Instead, it is at the very heart of this Handbook.

Cambridge, Massachusetts
July 2004

Contents

Decision Analysis

1. Introduction

Lawyers have to make all kinds of decisions — some of them quite complex — when conducting litigation or counseling clients. Obviously, lawyers and clients would like all their decisions to be the best ones possible. The surest way to reach this goal is by proceeding through the decision-making process in an organized and methodical way. Decision analysis provides a tool for doing just this. It's an organized method of making decisions — indeed, an enthusiast might even say that it is *the* rational way to go about making decisions — that is especially valuable when decisions have to be made in the face of uncertainty and when one decision must be followed by subsequent decisions.

Here are several typical decision-making problems of the types that you might encounter in your practice of law:

- *Automobile accident settlement negotiation.* You're the lawyer for a plaintiff who was in an automobile accident, and you're involved in settlement negotiation with the defendant's lawyer. If you go to trial, there will be three possible outcomes. First, you might win and prevail on the major issue of damages: lost wages. In this event, your client will receive a total award of $100,000. The likelihood of this outcome, in your opinion, is 50%. Second, your client may win at trial but not obtain lost wages. In this case, she'll receive only $20,000 for the damage to her car. You think that the chances of this outcome are 30%. Third, your client might lose at trial and thus win nothing. In your estimation, the probability that this will be the outcome is 20%. Going to trial would cost $10,000. The defendant has offered $40,000 to settle the case. Should you advise your client to accept this offer?

- *Land purchase decision.* Your client, who wishes to build a restaurant, is trying to decide which of two parcels of land to buy. Parcel A has been offered at $300,000 and Parcel B at only $250,000. They seem equally attractive, so your client initially thinks that purchasing the cheaper one, Parcel B, is the way to go. However, in questioning the sellers about the parcels, you learn that Parcel B may have an environmental problem because wastes have been dumped on it, whereas no problems are associated with Parcel A. You find that if the wastes on Parcel B are hazardous, the law would require your client to clean up the site and that the cost of cleanup would be $200,000. You figure that the odds of Parcel B having this problem are 50%. But before your client decides which parcel to buy, you can hire an environmental testing firm to determine definitively whether your client would have to clean up Parcel B. Having the environmental firm do the testing would cost your client $20,000. Should you advise your client to have the testing done? Or should he just buy Parcel A? Or Parcel B?

- *Tax deduction advice.* You're a tax lawyer advising a client about a tax matter and don't know whether a particular tax deduction — one that would save her $80,000 — is allowable (it's a judgment call that involves no ethical issue). If she takes the deduction, she'll be audited with probability 75% (she's in a group that's often audited for such deductions). If she's audited, the odds that the deduction will be found to be allowable are 50%. If she's audited and the deduction is disallowed, she won't obtain the $80,000 benefit, and she'll have to pay a penalty of $20,000. Should you advise her to claim the deduction?

- *Medical decision and negligence issue.* You are a lawyer helping a health maintenance organization formulate a medical treatment policy that will prevent it from being sued for negligence. For patients with a certain kind of heart ailment that will lead to immediate death if untreated, there are two options, both involving substantial risk. The first is a course of drug treatment, which will be successful 50% of the time but will also fail to prevent death 50% of the time. The second option is corrective surgery. The operation will be successful 33⅓% of the time. It won't go well and will result in patient death 10% of the time. The rest of the time it won't solve the problem and will leave the patient in a weakened condition. In this case, the patient's only option will be treatment with the drug, but now the drug has only a 25% chance of working. Neither the drug treatment nor the corrective surgery is very expensive in relation to any reasonable valuation of life, so it would be negligent not to choose some method of treatment. The question is, to avoid a finding of negligence, which method should be chosen (assuming that cost is not taken into consideration in the negligence determination)?

We'll use decision analysis to work through some of these problems, as well as some others, a little later in this Handbook. But, as an experiment, you might try to solve them right now on your own, if only to see how difficult the process sometimes can be.

Decision analysis is useful for a number of reasons. Some decisions are quite complicated to make — because of the number of choices, the number of possible consequences and their likelihoods, and the significance of decisions at each stage for later decisions. Therefore, more than intuition is often needed to see through to an answer, and decision analysis can fill this void.

Decision analysis is also useful because it forces us to be explicit about the considerations relevant to making a decision. It requires that we write down all the factors that might influence us. This process itself frequently yields significant dividends. In addition, listing all the potential consequences of a decision, assessing the likelihood of each, and noting all subsequent decisions that might have to be made down the road commonly reveals relevant issues and possibilities that would otherwise have been overlooked. In this regard, the sketches above may be a bit misleading, because the relevant events, their likelihoods, and future actions were laid out. In real life, we have to figure out for ourselves what they are.

As is obvious from the sketches, decision analysis can be relevant and helpful both to lawyers who are involved in active litigation and to lawyers who are advising clients before disputes arise. Much of the work that's necessary in making decisions to help clients is work that has to be done by lawyers: it is the lawyers who are often in the best position to identify many relevant contingencies, their likelihoods, and their significance. For instance, in the settlement negotiation sketch, the lawyer will have the best knowledge of the odds of winning this or that amount in the judgment. In the land purchase example, the lawyer might be the person who will be on the lookout for possible environmental problems (the environmental issue might not be on the radar screen of someone who doesn't purchase land very often), who will know what types of wastes have to be removed and precisely what the cleanup obligation entails, who will be familiar with waste-testing firms, and so forth. For such reasons, many lawyers themselves explicitly use decision analysis. Some hire consultants to teach them how to work through the decision analysis process. Others hire consultants to do the decision analyses.

Moreover, decision analysis is a mainstay of business and government decision making and is increasingly used in the medical world and in other arenas. A knowledge of decision analysis will prove useful to you in your practice not only because it will be of direct value to when you're making decisions but also because it will allow you to better understand the situation at hand and to communicate more effectively with your clients.

Box 1
Is Decision Analysis Ethical?

Is using decision analysis always ethical when doing so would be helpful to your client? For example, is employing decision analysis always ethical when giving tax advice? The answer, of course, is that your general ethical and legal obligations as a lawyer should guide you in providing advice to your client. There's nothing special per se about legal advice that makes use of decision analysis. Thus, if your client is seeking tax advice in the face of uncertainty about the interpretation of tax laws (as in our tax deduction example), decision analysis is good to employ. But if your client is trying to evade taxes clearly owed, it's wrong to knowingly aid your client, be it with decision analysis or in any other way.

2. Decision Trees

The first step in decision analysis is to convert a problem into a standard format: a *decision tree*. This format, which is quite intuitive, has proven to be very helpful. It displays all the decisions that are possible and all the consequences that are possible, along with their probabilities and their importance, the latter often being expressed in monetary terms. (How this information is obtained is another matter, which we'll explore a little later. For now, we'll assume that the decision maker has it.) Once a decision tree is displayed, it has to be solved. The process of solving a decision tree, like the format itself, is intuitive.

A. A Simple Problem

Let's begin by focusing on an extremely simple settlement decision. Suppose that your client is the plaintiff in a contract case. If he proceeds to trial, he will surely win, because the case is a slam-dunk: there was a clear breach of contract. The amount your client will receive if he goes to trial is $100,000, and legal costs will be $20,000, so your client will net $80,000. The defendant has offered your client $70,000.

The tree diagram for this scenario is shown in Figure 1. As we can see, it begins on the left with a box, a *decision node*. Two lines, referred to as *decision branches*, emanate from the box. They represent each of the two possible decisions that you can make: Settle (i.e., accept the settlement offer) and Trial (i.e., reject the offer and go to trial).[1] The $70,000 written along the Settle branch is the amount your client will receive if he settles. This is the *payoff*, or *consequence*, corresponding to the decision branch Settle. A negative amount, −$20,000, is noted along the Trial decision branch. This is the cost of going to trial. The payoff notation is followed by $100,000, the amount won at trial. Determining which

---

1. In a decision tree, the number of lines extending from a decision node always equals the number of decisions that are possible.

Figure 1
Settlement versus Trial

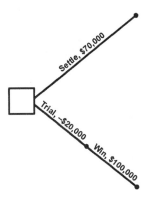

branch to choose, Settle or Trial, is readily apparent in this tree: if you settle, you get $70,000, and if you go to trial, you net $80,000. You would, obviously, choose Trial.

To indicate that a decision branch has been eliminated, we strike two lines through that line branch (see Figure 2). Similarly, the payoff when the best decision is made at a decision node is written underneath the decision node (e.g., the $80,000 in Figure 2).

Figure 2
Settlement versus Trial: The Best Decision

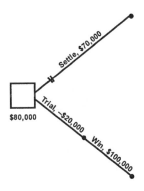

Striking off eliminated decision branches and recording under the decision node the best possible payoff is conventional practice in decision analysis. This practice may seem unnecessary to you at this point, but it proves to be very helpful when dealing with more complicated decision problems, as will soon become clear.

B. Uncertainty

Now let's introduce the element of uncertainty into our story. Suppose that your case for breach of contract is not a sure thing, because the other side has a possible counterargument. You think that the odds of prevailing at trial are only about 60%. If the decision doesn't come down on your side, your client will lose and collect nothing. This scenario is illustrated in Figure 3.

Notice that a circle is drawn at the end of the decision branch Trial. This circle, a *chance node*, signifies that chance will play a role in what next happens. In our example, your client either will

Figure 3
Settlement versus Trial: Uncertainty

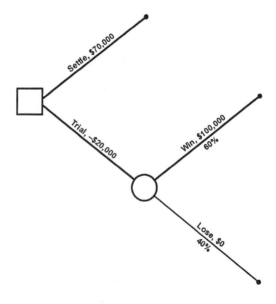

Win and gain $100,000 or will Lose and receive $0. Each outcome is indicated along a *chance branch,* and its likelihood is written under the branch. Thus, the tree diagram in Figure 3 contains all the relevant information provided by the verbal description of the problem.

Now that we have a visual representation of the problem, how do we evaluate the uncertain payoffs from trial? Let's focus on just a part of the decision tree, the uncertain chance branches for Trial (see Figure 4). How does it make sense to evaluate this situation, where there's a 60% chance of gaining $100,000 and a 40% chance of obtaining nothing? Plainly, if the chances of winning $100,000 were 100%, the evaluation of the situation would be $100,000. Just as clear is that, if the chances of winning anything were 0%, the evaluation of the situation would be $0. What we're confronted with, however, is a situation where you will Win with a probability of 60% and Lose with a probability of 40%. Intuition suggests that the evaluation of the situation should be somewhere between $100,000 and $0.

Figure 4
Chance Branches

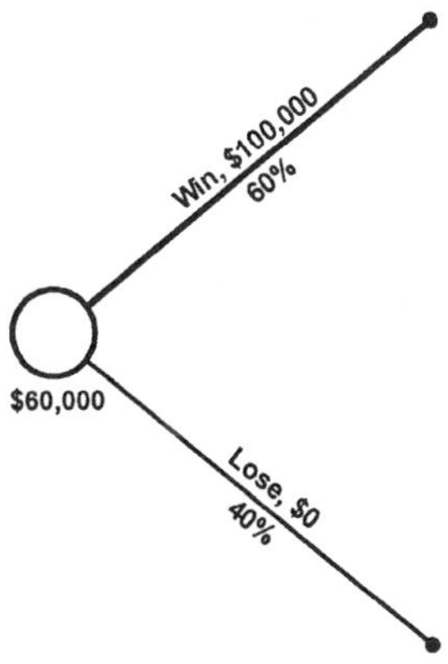

How do we decide what amount between $100,000 and $0 to use? The natural choice would seem to be the *expected value*, which is the probability of the payoff multiplied by the amount of the payoff. In this case, the expected value is $60,000 (i.e., 60% × $100,000 = $60,000). The expected value is the obvious, natural number to use as an evaluation because it is the average payoff a person would obtain if repeatedly faced with a risky situation similar to the type in question. Suppose that you find yourself repeatedly in trial situations in which you feel the odds of winning $100,000 are 60% (and the odds of winning $0 are 40%). You don't know what will happen in any one trial, of course, but you would know what your average winnings would be over the course of many of these trials: about $60,000. In other words, if you were to repeat the situation under discussion 100 times and anticipated obtaining $100,000 in 60 trials and gaining nothing in the other 40 trials,[2] your total gain would be $6,000,000 (i.e., 60 × $100,000 = $6,000,000), and thus your average gain would be $60,000 (i.e., $6,000,000/100 = $60,000).

For the time being, let's accept expected value as an appropriate measure or value of chance events and return to the decision tree in Figure 4. In this example, $60,000 is the expected value of the chance events following from the decision to go to trial, so we write $60,000 under the chance node. This notation indicates that we evaluate the chancy situation as if it were worth $60,000.

If we look again at the full decision tree, in Figure 5, we can see that we're now in a position to compare the two decision branches, Trial and Settle. It's apparent that Trial is worse than Settle. Trial requires an expenditure of $20,000 and leads to the chance node worth $60,000, yielding a net of $40,000, whereas Settle is worth

---

2. This distribution of trial outcomes, 60 and 40, is suggested by the probabilities 60% and 40%. The actual number of outcomes of each type might well be different, but usually the number of wins in 100 trials would be close to 60 if the likelihood of winning each is 60%.

Figure 5
Settlement versus Trial: Uncertainty and the Best Decision

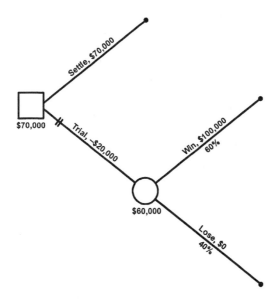

$70,000. Hence, Settle is the better decision. We therefore strike off the decision branch Trial, leaving Settle as the better of the two possible decisions that you can make with your client. We also note the payoff — $70,000 — under the first decision box to indicate that this is the amount that will be obtained if you make the best decision, Settle.

C. Risk Aversion

You might be thinking that your client wouldn't necessarily have assigned a $60,000 value to the chancy situation in which $100,000 is won with a 60% probability and $0 gained with a 40% probability. Perhaps your client is scared of the possibility of ending with nothing (in addition to having to spend $20,000 on litigation) and really needs to wind up with some positive amount of money. In such a case, your client would evaluate the chancy situation as worth less than $60,000, maybe only $50,000. A client who treats a risky situation as worth less than its expected value is called *risk averse,* and the lower the client's evaluation of the situation, the more risk averse the client is said to be.

Risk aversion is often relevant where the amounts in question are large in relation to a party's wealth and where the party might be left with low assets. It helps to explain why people like to purchase insurance. It also suggests why people ordinarily are reluctant to commit too much of their assets to one investment and, instead, tend to diversify. However, risk aversion would not necessarily be relevant where the amounts at stake don't constitute a significant proportion of a party's assets. For instance, risk aversion might not be relevant to a wealthy person or to a large corporation in litigation involving a sum like $100,000.

If risk aversion is relevant when you're using a decision tree, your evaluation of a chancy payoff should be a number lower than the expected value — for example, a number like $50,000 or $40,000, rather than $60,000 in our hypothetical case. You can use your intuition or judgment to arrive at an appropriate lower number.[3] Better yet, discuss it with your client.

Mainly for convenience, expected value will be used as the evaluation of risky situations in the material that follows.

D. Application: Settlement Negotiation

Let's go back to the first example described at the beginning of the chapter: settlement negotiation following an automobile accident. The decision tree, in Figure 6, is similar to the one for the contract case with an uncertain outcome that we just discussed.

The initial decision is whether to accept the settlement offer or to go to trial, so we begin with a decision node that has two deci-

---

3. Alternatively, you could use a more systematic approach to find the right lower number, which is often called the *certainty equivalent.* If you'd like to learn about this, be sure to check the sources mentioned in Section 5.

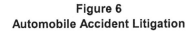

Figure 6
Automobile Accident Litigation

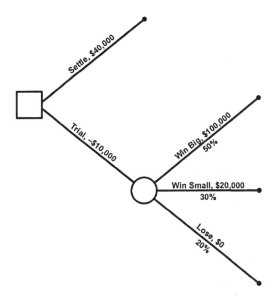

sion branches extending from it, Settle and Trial. Along the Settle decision branch, we write $40,000 as the payoff, which was stated to be the settlement offer. Along the Trial branch, we now write –$10,000, the stated legal expense of trial for this case. At the end of the Trial branch, we draw a chance node, because the outcome of trial is uncertain. There are three possible outcomes of going to trial in this example, so we must have three chance branches coming off the chance node. First, as indicated on the uppermost chance branch, the client can Win Big and obtain $100,000 in damages. The probability of this outcome is 50%. Second, as noted on the middle chance branch, the client can Win Small, receiving only $20,000. The likelihood that this would be the outcome is 30%. Third, as represented by the lowermost chance branch, the person may Lose and emerge from trial with nothing. The odds of this outcome are 20%. (It's worth noting again that the decision

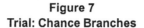

Figure 7
Trial: Chance Branches

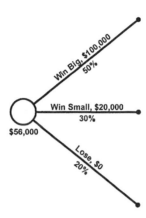

tree contains all the information that's in the verbal description and displays it in a fashion that shows the sequence in which decisions are made and events unfold.)

We solve this decision tree in much the same way that we solved the one in the contract case. Let's start by paying particular attention to the chance node and the chance branches corresponding to going to trial (see Figure 7). We have to figure out what the expected value is, taking into account the three possible outcomes: gaining $100,000 with a probability of 50%, gaining $20,000 with a probability of 30%, and losing with a probability of 20% (in other words, gaining $0 with a probability of 20%). As we can see from Table 1-1, the expected value is (50% × $100,000) + (30% × $20,000) + (20% × $0), or $56,000.[4] We can interpret this figure — $56,000 — as being the amount that your client would obtain, on average, after repeated litigation if your assessment of the odds of the three outcomes were those we used here. We record the expected value, $56,000, under the chance node.

_____

4. In general, the expected value of a risky situation with many possible payoffs is found as follows: multiply each payoff amount by its probability, and then add these figures.

Table 1
Computing the Expected Value

Chance Branch	Amount × Probability	= Product
Win Big	$100,000 × 50%	= $50,000
Win Small	$ 20,000 × 30%	= $ 6,000
Lose	$ 0 × 20%	= $ 0
	Expected value:	$56,000

The decision tree can be solved now, so let's return to the full tree as it appears in Figure 8, which includes all the information from Figure 7. Because $56,000 is the evaluation of the chance node following Trial, the evaluation of the branch Trial is $46,000 (i.e., $56,000 − $10,000 = $46,000). When we compare this amount ($46,000) with the value of Settle, $40,000, it's apparent that Trial is superior. So we strike off Settle and write $46,000 under the

Figure 8
Automobile Accident Litigation: The Best Decision

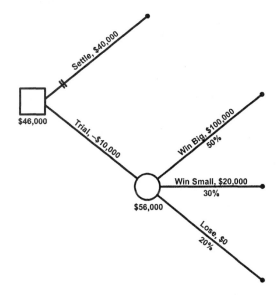

beginning decision node. We've solved this decision problem: Trial, with an evaluation of $46,000, is the better of the two possible decisions.[5]

E. Application: Land Purchase

We're now ready to tackle the land purchase decision outlined at the beginning of the section. Even though this problem is more complex than the ones we've already worked through, no new conceptual apparatus is required to solve it.

The first thing that we have to do is to translate the problem into decision-tree format. A good way to do this is to think about the problem in chronological order. Let's begin by determining what is the first decision that has to be made. Recall that your

Figure 9
The Initial Land Purchase Problem

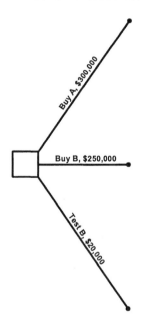

---

5. Consider how a highly risk-averse client might assess this situation.

client has to decide whether to purchase Parcel A or Parcel B and whether to test Parcel B for hazardous wastes. In other words, your client must, in fact, initially decide among three options. Hence, the decision tree begins with a decision box from which three decision branches emanate: Buy A, Buy B, and Test B. The additional labels in Figure 9 — $300,000, $250,000, and $20,000 — reflect, respectively, the purchase prices of Parcels A and B and the cost of testing Parcel B for hazardous wastes. (Minus signs aren't used here because all the outcomes are expenses and all the payoffs are written with this understanding in mind.)

Now we have to extend the tree to take into account what, if anything, happens after the initial decision is made. As we can see from Figure 10, a chance node follows decision branch Buy B, because one of two events will occur if your client decides to buy Parcel B: your client will discover that hazardous wastes have to be cleaned up or that hazardous wastes don't have to be cleaned up. So one possibility is Cleanup, which was said to involve an expense of $200,000, as indicated along with its probability of 50% on the upper chance branch. The other possibility, represented on the lower chance branch, is No Cleanup, which involves no additional expense and which also has a probability of 50%.

A chance node also follows decision branch Test B because testing for hazardous waste can result in either of two outcomes — Cleanup Required and No Cleanup Required — each of which, as noted in Figure 10, has a probability of 50%.

If testing results in Cleanup Required, your client likewise decides which parcel to buy, so another decision node is added to the tree. If your client chooses Buy A, the cost will, of course, be $300,000. If your client instead elects Buy B, the total cost will be $450,000: $250,000 (the price of Parcel B) plus $200,000 (the cost of cleaning up Parcel B) because cleanup is required.

If testing for hazardous wastes results in No Cleanup Required, your client likewise decides which parcel to buy, and a decision node with two branches is added: Buy A and Buy B. If your client opts for Buy A, the cost will be $300,000. If your client chooses

Figure 10
The Complete Land Purchase Problem

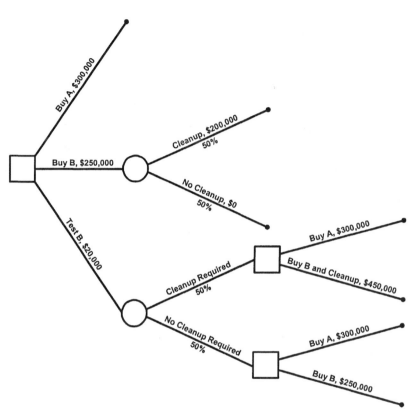

Box 2
The Value of Information

When we figure out whether testing for hazardous wastes is worthwhile, we'll be solving a problem of a pretty general type: is it worth paying a particular amount for information? Decision theory allows us to answer this question because it enables us to take into proper account how much better off we will be in light of how we would use the information we get.

Buy B, the cost will be the Parcel B purchase price — $250,000 — and no more, because the parcel doesn't have to be cleaned up.

Now that the decision tree reflects all the possible decisions that can be made and all the possible events that can occur, it can be solved.[6] Let's work through the solution, which appears in Figure 11. We begin with the topmost decision branch, Buy A. Evaluating this branch is straightforward: the cost is $300,000. In

Figure 11
The Land Purchase Problem: The Best Decisions

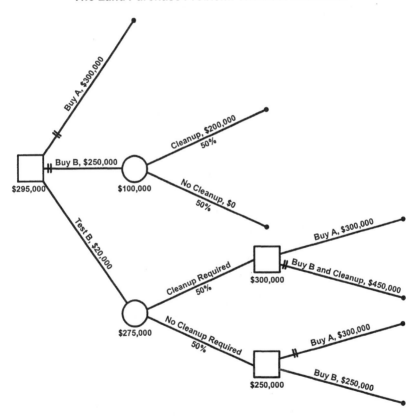

---

6. The tree could be drawn in a different way: it could begin with a choice between Test and Don't Test. Can you see how it would then continue? And can you verify that its solution is equivalent to what we find here?

evaluating decision branch Buy B, we have to consider the chance node following it. That is, we have to calculate the expected cleanup cost: 50% × $200,000 = $100,000. In other words, if Parcel B is purchased, the expected cleanup cost will be $100,000. So $100,000 is noted below the chance node. Consequently, if the client buys Parcel B, the evaluation is $350,000 (i.e., the $250,000 purchase price plus the $100,000 expected cleanup cost). The $350,000 evaluation exceeds the $300,000 cost of Buy A, so Buy B can be struck off because it's a worse decision than Buy A is. (As you can see, Buy A is also struck off in Figure 11. We'll get to the reason for this in a moment.)

Let's consider the remaining decision branch, Test B. Two possible chance outcomes follow this branch — Cleanup Required and No Cleanup Required — but we can't evaluate this chance node yet, because we haven't determined what decisions would be made later or their value. What we do in this situation is work backward. Starting with Cleanup Required, we see from the tree that Buy A is better than Buy B in this situation, because $300,000 is less than $450,000. This, of course, accords with the intuition that paying $300,000 for Parcel A is better than paying $250,000 for Parcel B and then having to spend an additional $200,000 to clean it up, bringing the total cost of Parcel B up to $450,000. Given that Buy A is the optimal decision in this case, Buy B is struck off and $300,000 is noted under the decision node.

Now for the other possibility, a test result of No Cleanup Required: Buy B is better than Buy A, because $250,000 is less than $300,000. In other words, paying $250,000 for Parcel B (which we know in this situation doesn't require cleaning up) is better than paying $300,000 for Parcel A. Because Buy B is the optimal decision, Buy A is struck off, and $250,000 is written under the decision node.

We're now in a position to evaluate the chance node that follows Test B. The evaluation is $300,000 for a test outcome of Cleanup Required and $250,000 for a test outcome of No Cleanup Required. So the expected value of the decision node following

---

Box 3
Government Policy Design and Decision Analysis

Suppose that the EPA often wants people (and corporations) to test land for hazardous wastes so that they'll undertake cleanup right away if hazardous wastes are found. Does the government have to subsidize testing or give tax credits for such testing in order to motivate people to do the testing? The EPA can find out whether people will want to test for hazardous wastes, given the current cost of testing, by using decision analysis. More generally, decision analysis can help government to predict people's behavior and thus enable government to design its policies intelligently.

Test B is \$275,000 — i.e., (50% × \$300,000) + (50% × \$250,000) = \$275,000 — and this figure is written under the chance node.

Finally, we have the information we need to evaluate decision branch Test B. The evaluation is \$295,000 (i.e., \$20,000 to perform the test and an expected payout of \$275,000 once the test is completed). This figure is lower than the \$300,000 evaluation of Buy A, so the Buy A decision is inferior and thus can be struck off. Hence, Test B emerges as the optimal decision, and \$295,000 — the expected value of the Test B decision — is noted under the first decision node.

At this point, it's worth stepping back for a moment to look at what we've just done in solving this problem and to put some kind of perspective on it.

First, not only have we found the best initial decision for you and your client to make — Test B — but we've also formulated a complete set of instructions for what you're supposed to do throughout the process. We can see this by examining the tree and going down the decision branches that aren't struck off. Specifically, you begin by choosing Test B, because the other two decision branches are struck off. Then you find out whether or not cleanup is needed. You're now at one or the other of the two decision nodes at the bottom right of the tree. For each of these, only one buy decision is available, the other having been struck off, so you can tell from the tree what your client should do: buy Parcel A or buy Parcel B, depending on whether or not toxic wastes have to be cleaned up from Parcel B.

Second, if you reflect on what we did to evaluate the Test B decision branch, you'll realize that we started at the right-most aspect of the tree and worked leftward. And we did this naturally, intuitively. Indeed, we had to work this way. For example, we couldn't know how to evaluate Cleanup Required without knowing whether your client would ultimately purchase Parcel A or Parcel B after the testing results were known for Cleanup Required. And we couldn't evaluate the Test B branch without knowing what decision you and your client would later make about purchasing for each of the possible test results. We had to do this because, in effect, we have to *look before we leap* in order to know what to do.

F. Generalizations

Some generalizations that are applicable in solving any decision tree can be derived from what we've done in the preceding examples:

> • Start at the right side of the tree — that is, with the last group of chance events or last group of decisions. (It doesn't matter where on the right side you begin.) Where there are chance events at the right end of the tree — that is, branches stemming from a chance node — compute the expected value, and write it under the chance node. Where a decision has to be made at the right end of the tree, figure out what decision is the best one, and strike off the other possibilities to indicate that you've

ruled them out. Be sure to write the value of the best decision under the decision node.

- Repeat this process for all of the right-most decision and chance nodes.
- Move one level to the left, repeat the preceding steps, and keep working leftward until you've finished with the tree.

One point that merits emphasis is truly good news: you really can't do the wrong thing in solving a decision tree, because it's impossible to evaluate any node without having already evaluated everything to the right of it. So, in a sense, you don't have to remember the specific technique described here. By simply attacking the tree, you will automatically be led to proceed from right to left, thereby reaching the correct solution.

G. Test Your Skill

Let's consider one more example of a decision-making problem, one more complicated than those we've already solved. If you can follow how this one is translated into a decision tree — and most likely you can — then you'll know that you have a good grasp of how to construct trees.

Suppose that you're advising a plaintiff and you're unsure about the magnitude of her losses (say, losses due to lost business resulting from a breach of contract). You can hire an expert to obtain a preliminary estimate of losses, and you figure that the preliminary estimate has an equal probability of being low ($200,000) or high ($400,000). The cost of hiring the expert is $20,000.

You'll have time before trial to develop support for the expert's estimates, but doing so will be costly. Specifically, if you spend $10,000 on supporting the low estimate, you'll receive $200,000 at trial for sure, whereas if you don't spend the $10,000, you'll have only a 50% chance of receiving $200,000 and a 50% chance of receiving $150,000. Similarly, if you spend $10,000 on supporting the high estimate, the probability is 80% that you'll receive $400,000 and 20% that you'll receive $350,000, whereas if you don't spend the $10,000, the odds are 70% that you'll receive $400,000 and 30% that you'll receive $350,000.

If you don't hire an expert, you won't have time before trial to support the estimate because you'll have no real idea of what the losses are and no guidance from an expert as to what facts you should try to demonstrate. You figure that, in this situation, trial has a 50% chance of resulting in a $150,000 judgment and a 50% chance of resulting in a $350,000 judgment, depending on the information revealed at the time of trial.

What should you do? The answer can be derived from the decision tree in Figure 12. This tree has two initial decisions branches: Hire Expert and No Expert.

Let's begin with the upper branch: Hire Expert. A cost of $20,000 is incurred, so this figure is noted on the branch. A chance node follows the branch, and it indicates the two possible estimates that the expert can discover: Low Estimate, which is $200,000, and High Estimate, which is $400,000. Their probabilities, 50% each, are noted on the chance branches. The decision node at the end of each chance branch indicates that a decision is to be made. The possibilities are Spend, $10,000 (i.e., spend $10,000 on trial preparation) and Don't Spend (i.e., spend nothing on trial preparation). If the expert reports the low estimate and you then opt to spend $10,000 on trial preparation, you're certain to win $200,000. If, on the other hand, you get the low estimate from the expert but don't spend on trial preparation, you might receive $200,000, but you're equally likely to get only $150,000, as indicated at the chance node that follows the Don't Spend decision branch.

We've just worked through the Hire Expert, Low Estimate part of the tree. The part just below — the Hire Expert, High Estimate section — is very similar. We're left with the No Expert decision branch. This branch is followed by a chance node from which two possibilities emanate: receiving $150,000 and receiving $350,000, each of which has a probability of 50%.

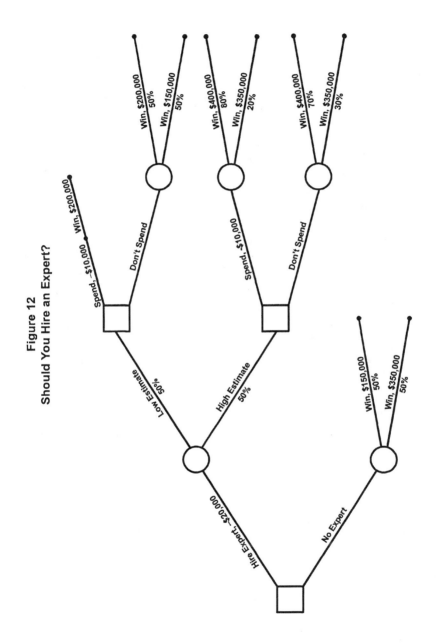

Figure 12
Should You Hire an Expert?

At this point, solving the tree should be straightforward. You might want to give it a try, either now or at a later time, as a review exercise. As you do so, see whether you can explain to yourself the intuition behind the best decisions to make.

3. Acquiring the Necessary Information

In the foregoing examples, the information needed to construct the decision trees was provided to us. We didn't have to gather it or develop it. But, in real life, being presented with such neat thumbnail sketches isn't at all typical. In fact, much of the information pertinent to making a decision often isn't readily available. And not all of the possible decisions may be obvious, because no one has methodically worked them out. So how can you, in your practice of law, get your hands on the information you need?

If we analyze the decision analysis process, we find that the information you'll require is of three basic types: (1) descriptions of the possible decisions and possible outcomes — in other words, information relevant to the structure of the decision tree; (2) the probabilities of the various chance events that are part of the tree; and (3) the numerical (or other) payoffs or costs associated with all the options.

A. Structure

Before you can do anything else, you'll have to ascertain the structure of the problem facing you. You'll have to identify the initial decision, determine what can happen as a result of each possibility, and so on. You may do this yourself. More often, though, the information will emerge from discussions with others, notably, with your client and sometimes with your lawyer colleagues, experts, and others. The process of describing the problem will frequently proceed chronologically, from the left of the decision tree to the right. This exercise will often provide a great deal of clarity, because it will force you — indeed, impose an inescapable discipline on you — to be precise and reasonably complete.

As pointed out earlier, your legal knowledge and your practical experience as a lawyer will play an important role in the structuring of the decision tree. If, for example, the problem at hand involves regulatory rules, you'll know them or learn them. If it involves potential liability for negligence, you'll know how the standard of care is determined. If it involves the conduct of litigation, you'll know about the pertinent legal procedure (e.g., the motions that might be filed, the discovery process, and trial itself). Frequently, you'll have, in addition, experience that your client doesn't have but that is relevant even though, strictly speaking, it isn't legal experience. For instance, you'll be aware that there are firms that test for hazardous wastes on land if you've already done many land transactions (and you'll know of specific firms that do such testing), whereas your client, having been involved in few, if any, transactions of this kind, may well be unaware that testing firms even exist (or even that testing for hazardous wastes may be necessary or desirable).

Another common benefit of formally constructing a decision tree is also worth noting: it may reveal that the number of possible decisions and the number of possible outcomes is greater than was originally thought. (However, you'll sometimes want to do a bit of simplifying and consolidating, especially of outcomes, to prevent the tree from becoming unwieldy.)

B. Probabilities

Once you've worked out the structure of the decision tree, you'll need to plug in the probabilities of events. But how will you figure out what the probabilities are? In some cases, you'll have access to hard data that are helpful. For instance, for the probability that you'll win a particular case, you might use the percentage of similar cases in which your side has prevailed. Similarly, in giving tax advice, you might use the audit rate. In other cases, relevant data won't be immediately available, but you'll have an opportunity to obtain it at some cost. For example, you might conduct mock trials to help predict the odds of winning at trial, or

---

Box 4
How Are Probabilities Determined in Practice?

Probabilities are often found by asking people to compare bets, just as described in the text. In fact, one very successful consultant uses a "betting wheel" that has an adjustable red wedge, which represents the "winning" area, and a black background, which represents the "losing" area. A lawyer starts with just a thin sliver of red and asks his client if she thinks the outcome in question is more likely to occur than the thin sliver of red would be to come up on a spin of the betting wheel. If she says no, he makes the red wedge progressively larger until she says, "Gee, I guess my outcome is about as likely to occur as the red wedge now is to come up on a spin of the betting wheel."

---

you might hire an expert to ascertain the likelihood that your client's conduct constituted negligence.

Often, however, you'll have to rely on subjective judgments in formulating probabilities. When trying to determine the likelihood of winning a case, you might find that data on very similar cases are insufficient or lacking altogether. You might not be able to locate information that would enable you to estimate the likelihood that the other party to a contract will breach it. In situations like these, probability estimates are unavoidably subjective. But, you might be asking, how can a specific probability be derived for use in such cases?

This question is most easily answered by example. Let's say that you're trying to ascertain the probability that you'll win a particular case. You can start by asking yourself, Would I prefer to place a bet in which I collect if I win my case or to place a bet in which I collect if any number between 1 and 30 turns up when a fair roulette wheel with 100 numbers on it is spun? If your answer is that you prefer the bet on your case, your subjective

---

Box 5
Time, Hassle, and Other Nonmonetary Payoffs

Don't forget to include in your assessment of payoffs factors that aren't purely financial. Various decisions and outcomes will involve the expenditure of time, which you'll definitely want to take into account and probably convert to some monetary equivalent. Another example: a client might want to avoid the emotional cost of trial or embarrassment of some type. You'll want to take a stab, with the help of your client, at incorporating such nonmonetary elements into your figures: a guesstimate is a lot better than ignoring these often important factors.

---

probability of winning is greater than 30%. If so, compare the bet on your case to a bet on the roulette wheel in which you win if any number between 1 and 40 comes up. If you still prefer the bet on your case, this means that you feel the odds of winning exceed 40%. Continue doing this type of comparison, adjusting the range of winning numbers on the roulette wheel up or down, until you reach a resting point — the point where you're indifferent between the bet on your case and the bet on the roulette wheel. This will tell you what your subjective probability is. For example, if you're indifferent between a bet on your case and a bet on the roulette wheel when any number between 1 and 60 turns up, your subjective probability of winning the case is 60%. Two points are worth noting about this method. First, even though it's subjective — a matter of your opinion — the result is influenced by the information you have. Second, you and others who use it might arrive at similar subjective probability estimates. And, when you don't, the discussion produced by your disagreement will often be illuminating and should provide a basis for formulating your best estimate.

You should keep in mind that many probabilities are ones that you, as the lawyer, will have to supply or have your client produce. Probabilities pertaining to legal outcomes are ones that you'll have to provide (or, at the least, play an important role in furnishing). It will be your responsibility to determine the odds of prevailing in a case or on an element of a case. Your client will be able to bring certain types of facts to the table that, in combination with your knowledge, will make it possible to arrive at probabilistic judgments about what will happen.

C. Payoffs

Payoffs (and costs) can be estimated by methods similar to those used in determining probabilities. You'll often find yourself obtaining information from clients to estimate payoffs and hiring experts to refine your estimates. Again, as a lawyer, you will have unique information to contribute. For instance, in determining payoffs in the form of possible damage awards, your knowledge of which elements of losses are included as damages will be relevant. You will also, in contrast to most of your clients, know such things as the costs of legal services and of various types of experts.

4. Sensitivity Analysis

As is probably evident by now, a recurring problem in constructing and solving decision trees is the problem of finding estimates for probabilities and final outcomes that are sufficiently reliable to make us feel reasonably confident in the outcomes of our analyses. Sometimes even our best efforts fail to yield a numerical estimate that we feel comfortable about. In such cases, it's natural to ask whether our decisions would be affected if the data on which they're based changed. Would we make a different decision if our probability assessments were different by some amount or if the profits we wrote down were altered by some amount? In considering this type of question, we're engaging in *sensitivity analysis*. This analysis process is so named because its object is to find out whether the best decision is sensitive to particular changes in the estimates.

One way of ascertaining how sensitive our answer is to the estimates is by asking how much our estimate of a probability or a payoff amount can vary without changing what we've found to be the best set of decisions. Sometimes we'll find that the optimal decision remains the same over a wide range of plausible estimates for the value under consideration. In other words, the decision is robust with respect to that value. In other cases, however, we'll find that even a small change in an estimated value leads to a different preferred decision. In cases of this type, we have good reason to seek further information in an attempt to improve our estimates.

Let's return to the problem represented in the first decision tree we looked at to see how sensitivity analysis works (see Figure 13). As pointed out earlier, the correct solution is trivial as long as you accept these estimates as accurate. Suppose, however, that you have reason to doubt the accuracy of the estimate of net recovery if you go to trial. Perhaps the expense of going to trial depends in part on how vigorously the defendant opposes you. Perhaps a jury wouldn't award the predicted amount. You'd want to know how far off your estimate of net recovery would have to

Figure 13
Settlement versus Trial: The Best Decision

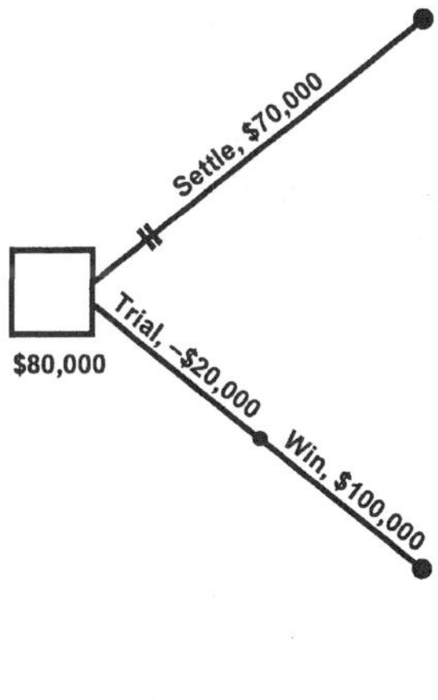

be for you to change your decision from Trial to Settle. The answer is obvious. Only if you reduced your estimate of the trial outcome from $100,000 to less than $90,000, which reduces the net recovery from $80,000 to less than $70,000 (i.e., the settlement offer), would you change your decision. Thus, an estimate of a trial outcome of $90,000, for a net recovery of $70,000, is a *crossover point* for the sensitivity analysis. In other words, if you cross over this point, you're going to change your decision. Crossover points often become focal points for reflection on the reliability of decision analyses.

Suppose that you can spend money to refine your information and that, in doing so, you might end up with information that would cause you to change one or more of your decisions. You can determine whether you should obtain the additional information (which itself is a decision problem, similar to the land purchase problem) in the following way: First, ascertain what your expected payoff is without having more information. Second, calculate what your expected payoff would be if you had the additional information (realizing that your best decision will generally depend on the type of information that you obtain). Finally, if this second value (the expected payoff with information) exceeds the first value (the expected payoff without information) by more than the cost of the information, you should obtain the information.

To illustrate, consider again the decision tree in Figure 13 and suppose that, right now, you're uncertain about the amount you would recover at trial. You think that you have a 50% probability of winning $150,000 and a 50% probability of winning only $50,000. You can, however, at a cost of $10,000 hire an expert on damages in advance to determine for sure whether you'd collect $50,000 or $150,000 at trial. See if you can construct a decision tree reflecting this situation and can use it to verify the following: If you don't hire the expert, your expected payoff is $80,000. If you hire the expert and he tells you that you would win $50,000 at trial, you would net $30,000 from trial, so you would decide to take the settlement of $70,000. If the expert tells you that you would win $150,000 at trial, you would net $130,000 from trial, so you would choose to go to trial. The expert's advice therefore increases your expected payoff from $80,000 to $100,000. Hiring the expert costs only $10,000, so it's desirable for you to do so.

5. Suggestions for Further Reading

If you're interested in delving further into decision analysis, there are a number of good treatments that you can turn to. An excellent presentation is set forth by George E. Monahan in *Management Decision Making* (Cambridge: Cambridge University Press, 2000), chapter 10. This chapter is intended as an introduction to decision analysis for graduate students in business. Robert T. Clemen's textbook, *Making Hard Decisions: An Introduction to Decision Analysis*, 2nd ed. (Pacific Grove, Calif.: Duxbury Press, 1996), is very good. You should be aware that the conventions used in decision trees can vary somewhat among publications (e.g., payoffs may be written either along branches of the tree, as we've done, or only at the end of the tree). All in all, however, what you'll come across is quite similar to the format we've used. Another recommendation is TreeAge Software's website, www.TreeAge.com, where you can find software that facilitates drawing and solving complex decision trees.

Some students may be interested in a classic by one of the founders of decision analysis, Howard Raiffa's *Decision Analysis* (Reading, Mass.: Addison-Wesley, 1968), or in the advanced-level texts, Detlof von Winterfeldt and Ward Edwards, *Decision Analysis and Behavioral Research* (Cambridge: Cambridge University Press, 1986), Ralph Keeney and Howard Raiffa, *Decisions with Multiple Objectives: Preferences and Value Tradeoffs* (New York: Wiley, 1976), and Howard Raiffa, John Richardson, and David Metcalfe, *Negotiation Analysis: The Science and Art of Collaborative Decision Making* (Cambridge, MA: Harvard University Press, 2003). Current academic work can be found in *Theory and Decision*, a multidisciplinary journal that's accessible to the general scholary audience.

A wealth of resources, including a guide to software and a huge bibliography (it contains more than a thousand entries) of books and articles on the subject, can be found at the website of the Decision Analysis Society (the professional organization of decision analysts), http://faculty.fuqua.duke.edu/daweb/.

Games and Information

1. Introduction to Game Theory

In many situations, people decide on an action based in part on how others are likely to act, on how they themselves are likely to react to the actions of others, or both. This is often true of actions chosen by players in many games. A chess player decides which piece to move and where to move it on the basis of what he anticipates his opponent's response will be. Similarly, in business, legal, and social interactions, parties frequently take into account the anticipated behavior of others when making their decisions. The price that an airline chooses to set on a particular route depends on whether it expects competitors to match or undercut its price. Whether a lawyer files a motion will depend on what she thinks the opposing side will do as a consequence of the motion. In deciding whether to extend a dinner invitation to someone, the host will take into account how he expects the person to behave at the party and whether the invitee is likely to reciprocate.

Game theory deals with such situations. The foundations of this discipline were laid in the 1920s and 1930s, and the study of military tactics during World War II stimulated its development. Game theory, now highly developed, provides a useful, flexible way to organize thinking about strategic decision making. For lawyers, it's valuable for these general reasons and for the aid it furnishes in designing contracts, formulating litigation strategy, and conducting all sorts of negotiation. In addition, a knowledge of game theory is a prerequisite to understanding much writing in law as well as areas of business of interest to lawyers, such as corporate takeovers and anticompetitive behavior.

2. Description of Games

A game involves *players.* In many cases, there are two players, as in a chess game or a legal case involving a plaintiff and a defendant. But sometimes there are more than two, as in some poker games, a legal case involving a plaintiff and two defendants, or three airlines competing on a route.

Each player chooses one or more *actions,* which can be anything from moving a chess piece to filing a legal motion to setting the price to charge for an item. The actions available to a player may vary over time. For instance, a chess player is able to move only pawns and knights at the beginning of a game but can move other pieces as well several moves later.[7]

Each player also has certain *information.* This, too, may change during the course of a game. For instance, the defendant might have little knowledge about the plaintiff's losses at the outset, whereas after discovery he might have substantial information about the plaintiff's losses.

The *timing* and *order of moves* are important aspects of games. The players often move after one another. For instance, chess players alternate moves. In litigation, if the plaintiff decides to file suit (the first move), the defendant then either files an opposing motion or offers to settle for some amount, and so forth. Sometimes, however, the parties act simultaneously or choose acts without knowing what acts the others are selecting. Consider, for instance, sealed bids submitted at auction or pleadings that opposing litigants are required to furnish to the court at the same time.

The objective of each player is to end up with the maximum possible *payoff.* Payoffs encompass all things that matter to a player, positively or negatively, at any time during the game. For instance, in litigation, payoffs include not only any payment that

---

7. In game theory, a *strategy* is a plan that specifies the action to be chosen at every possible juncture. In chess, for instance, a strategy would tell you what

the litigant ultimately makes or receives through settlement or trial judgment but also the time and money that she expends as well as any pleasure or displeasure that she experiences from the negotiation or trial process.

One device that's sometimes useful when working with games, especially when two players are involved, is the *game table*. The easiest way to explain a game table is by example. Let's suppose the following: (1) Amy and Bill are two opposing litigants, each of whom claims ownership of some asset, say, from an inheritance. (2) Amy can choose one of two actions: Discovery or No Discovery. (3) Bill can select one of three actions: Expert Witness (hire an expert witness), Consultant (hire just a consultant), or Do Nothing. A game table representing this situation can be created, as in Table 1, by assigning each of Amy's possible actions (Discovery and No Discovery) to a row and each of Bill's possible actions (Expert Witness, Consultant, and Do Nothing) to a column. Then, a particular cell in the game table corresponds to one of Amy's possible actions and one of Bill's possible actions. For instance, the cell in the first row and the first column corresponds to Amy's choosing Discovery and Bill's choosing Expert Witness. In general, the payoff to each player will depend on the action that each takes. The players in a game are presumed to know (or to estimate) the payoffs they would get as a result of their actions.

How are the payoffs written in the game table? In each cell, the payoffs for the players are written for the actions of that cell. By convention, the payoff of the player whose actions are listed to the left (in Table 1, this would be Amy's payoff) is the first num-

Table 1
Game Table: Bill and Amy

		Bill's Action		
		Expert Witness	Consultant	Do Nothing
Amy's	Discovery	3, 4	5, 7	9, 2
Action	No Discovery	2, 10	8, 8	12, 4

ber in the cell, and the payoff of the player whose actions are listed at the top (in Table 1, Bill's payoff) is the second number. So, if Amy chooses No Discovery and Bill chooses Expert Witness, the bottom left cell tells us that they get 2 and 10, respectively. Similarly, if Amy chooses Discovery and Bill chooses Consultant, Amy gets 5 and Bill gets 7, according to the entry in the top center cell.

A famous example of a game that can be represented by a table is the *prisoners' dilemma*. In this game, there are two prisoners, Baxter and Chester, who in fact are guilty of a theft. They are questioned separately. If both confess, each will be sentenced to 10 years in prison. If both deny their guilt, each will be sentenced to 1 year in prison, because the prosecution will be able to prove only a lesser offense. If one confesses and the other denies guilt, the deal with the prosecutor will be that the one who confesses will go free, and the other will receive a 15-year sentence. In this game, both players have the same two options — Confess to the theft or Deny guilt — and payoffs are measured in number of years in prison (see Table 2).[8] Note that, in each cell, the first payoff is Chester's (because it's his possible actions that are listed on the left), and Baxter's payoff is written second. Thus, if Chester chooses Confess and Baxter opts for Deny, Chester gets off scot-free and Baxter goes to jail for 15 years, so the payoffs are entered as 0, 15. (We'll return to Chester and Baxter a little later to figure out what they might be expected to do.)

Game trees, which are similar to decision trees, provide an alternative way of representing games. They're especially helpful when players' actions are sequential. Again, let's consider a simple example. Suppose that a victim suffers a loss and can choose either of two actions: Sue or Lump It (do nothing and just accept the loss). If the victim sues, suppose that the defendant, in turn, can choose either of two actions: Settle (settle the suit for what the plaintiff asks — we're simplifying here) or Go to Trial. The

---

8. The payoffs could have been written as negative numbers rather than as positive numbers.

Table 2
Game Table: The Prisoners' Dilemma

		Baxter's Action	
		Confess	Deny
Chester's	Confess	10, 10	0, 15
Action	Deny	15, 0	1, 1

tree representing the game tree to this point appears in Figure 1. Note that the initial box — a *decision node* — is labeled P (short for *plaintiff*), because it's the plaintiff who first chooses an action (in this case, either Sue or Lump It).[9] Each possible decision is indicated by a *decision branch*. At the end of the Sue branch, there's another decision node. This one is marked D (for *defendant*), because the defendant has a decision to make at this point if the plaintiff has filed suit. The two possible actions are Settle and Go to Trial, each with its own decision branch. After the defendant makes this choice, whichever action it is, the game ends.

It's worth noting that this game, as simple as it is, can't be represented by a game table. The reason is that, in a table, each possible action of one player appears in combination with *each* possible action of the other player. But this isn't the case here. Lump It can't, for example, be paired with Go to Trial; the combination makes no sense. The defendant's possible actions — Settle and Go to Trial — are available for consideration *only* if the plaintiff has chosen Sue. A table in which possible actions are arranged in rows and columns doesn't allow for the representation of situations where players move in sequence and the action of one player subsequently affects the set of actions available to the other player.

Continuing with our example, let's say that it was the plaintiff's loss of $10,000 in an accident that gave rise to the game, and let's

_____

9. As you'll recall from the Decision Analysis section, we don't label decision nodes when we construct decision trees. Doing so is unnecessary because

Figure 1
A Simple Litigation Game Tree

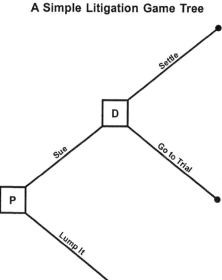

assume that filing suit would cost the plaintiff $3,000, that the defendant would pay $8,000 if the case were settled, and that each side would bear $2,000 in expenses and the judgment would be for $9,000 if the case went to trial.[10]

Payoffs can be incorporated into a game tree as shown in Figure 2. Any payoff associated with a possible action is noted along the corresponding decision branch, and the accumulated, final payoffs (i.e., the net payoffs) for each possible pathway are written next to the decision node representing the end of the game for that pathway. By convention, the plaintiff's payoff is entered first, because he moves first, and the defendant's payoff is entered second, because he moves second.

For example, in Figure 2, the first amount at the uppermost end node of the tree (the one following Settle) is $5,000. This would be

---

10. The plaintiff might, for example, not be able to establish $1,000 of his loss. Hence, the judgment would be for only $9,000 rather than the full $10,000 loss. These amounts are the payoffs for this game.

Figure 2
A Simple Litigation Game Tree with Payoffs

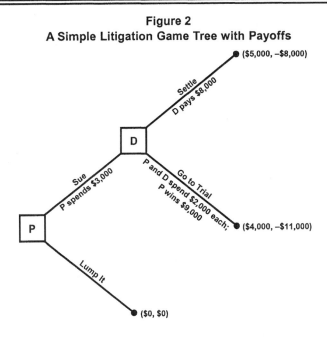

the plaintiff's payoff — the amount that she would end with (i.e., if she spent $3,000 to file suit and received $8,000 in a settlement, her net return would be $5,000).[11] The second amount written after the same end node is –$8,000, which would be the defendant's payoff. It's written as a negative number because he spends $8,000 on the settlement. Similarly, at the next end node (the one after Go to Trial), the plaintiff's payoff is $4,000 (i.e., she would spend $3,000 to file suit and $2,000 to go to trial and would obtain a judgment of $9,000), and the defendant's payoff is –$11,000 (i.e., he would spend $2,000 on trial and $9,000 on the judgment). At the bottom end node (after Lump It), because neither the plaintiff nor the defendant would pay or receive anything, the payoff for

---

11. For convenience, we've disregarded the $10,000 loss that the plaintiff sustained before the game began. We took into account only amounts spent or received during the game. However, it would be all right to add in to each of the plaintiff's final payoffs the amount the plaintiff had when the game began.

each is $0.[12]

Chance plays a role in many games, and it, too, can be reflected in game trees, in much the same way that it is in the decision trees of the Decision Analysis section. For example, perhaps a $9,000 outcome isn't a certainty for the plaintiff in our example if she goes to trial. Perhaps, instead, she has a two-thirds probability of winning and receiving the $9,000 and a one-third probability of losing and receiving nothing.

The tree in Figure 3 (a modified version of the one in Figure 2) shows how such a situation can be represented. A *chance node* follows the Go to Trial branch, and two *chance branches* extend from this node. The probability of each outcome is written under the corresponding branch: ⅔ for P Wins $9,000 and ⅓ for P Loses. And, as before, the final payoffs for the plaintiff and the defendant are noted at the end nodes following the branches: $4,000 for the plaintiff and −$11,000 for the defendant after P Wins $9,000, and −$5,000 for the plaintiff (i.e., the net after spending $3,000 to file suit and $2,000 to go to trial) and −$2,000 for the defendant (i.e., all he spends is $2,000 in trial) after P Loses.

It should be apparent from the foregoing discussion that trees provide a great deal of flexibility for the representation of games.

3. Solving Games

Solving a game means figuring out what each player will do if he's rational. In effect, then, solving a game is making a prediction about what will happen when each player tries to achieve the outcome that's the best one for himself. Let's begin by working through the prisoners' dilemma. To see how this is done, let's start by looking again at Table 2.

---

12. A point about game trees that's worth keeping in mind is that the payoffs are not always indicated along the way, but including them at the end nodes is conventional. Another point to note is that, in the decision trees that we considered in the Decision Analysis section, we didn't write down accumulated payoffs at the end nodes, although some analysts do so.

Figure 3
A Litigation Game Tree

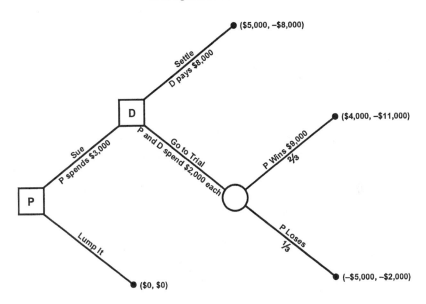

For Chester, Confess is better than Deny, no matter what action Baxter selects: *if Baxter confesses,* Chester is better off confessing than denying because his sentence will be 10 years rather than 15 years; *if Baxter denies guilt,* Chester is better off confessing because he'll end up with no sentence rather than with a 1-year sentence. Likewise for Baxter, Confess is better than Deny, regardless of Chester's action: *if Chester confesses,* Baxter is better off confessing than denying because he'll be sentenced to 10 years rather than 15 years; *if Chester denies,* Baxter is better off confessing because he'll get no sentence rather than a 1-year sentence. Hence, both Chester and Baxter will choose Confess. Now that we've figured out what Chester's and Baxter's decisions will be, we can determine the outcome of the game: each will receive a 10-year sentence.

Table 2
Game Table: The Prisoners' Dilemma

		Baxter's Action	
		Confess	Deny
Chester's Action	Confess	10, 10	0, 15
	Deny	15, 0	1, 1

You may have noticed that the outcome could have been better for both Chester and Baxter. If both had chosen Deny, the sentence for each would have been 1 year rather than 10 years, which we arrived at in solving the game. The game is said to be a dilemma for the prisoners because they jointly make themselves worse off when each attempts to pursue his interest.

Of the two possible actions open to each player in the prisoners' dilemma game, one is the best for the player to choose regardless of the action selected by the other player. In other words, a *dominant strategy* is available to each player, and this is the one — Confess — that the player selects. In such situations, where each player has a dominant strategy, games are easy to

---

Box 1
Why Is the Prisoners' Dilemma So Important?

The prisoners' dilemma represents a very typical problem: one in which people wind up in a bad situation relative to where they could be had they *cooperated* in their actions. Do you understand why the following might — or might not — be considered (by some) to be the undesirable outcomes of prisoners' dilemmas?

- Athletes take harmful drugs, such as steroids, to boost their performance.
- Countries engage in an arms race.
- Students study hard for exams.

solve. In many games, however, there are no dominant strategies. What is best for a given player to do depends on what the other player does.

Let's reconsider the game in which Amy and Bill are the players (see Table 1). Amy has no dominant strategy: for example, she's better off choosing Discovery if Bill chooses Expert Witness but No Discovery if Bill chooses Consultant. (Can you explain why?) Nor does Bill have a dominant strategy: his best option is Consultant if Amy selects Discovery but Expert Witness if she selects

---

Box 2
How Can the Prisoners Get Out of Their Dilemma?

If the prisoners could communicate with each other to coordinate their strategy and somehow commit themselves to deny their guilt, they'd get the outcome they want. Another possibility is that both have developed in past encounters a reputation for denying guilt, so each would expect the other to continue to do so. A great deal of discussion in game theory literature revolves around these two avenues of escaping the bad outcome of the prisoners' dilemma.

No Discovery. (Can you explain why?[13]) Thus, for Amy and for Bill, the best action depends on what the other one does.

Another simple example of a game in which players don't have dominant strategies concerns which side of the road a driver would choose to drive on (were there no traffic laws). Clearly, if everyone else drives on the right, the best action for the driver in question is to drive on the right, in order to avoid accidents. On the other hand, if everyone else drives on the left, the best action

---

13. You should also explain why Bill will rule out Do Nothing.

Table 1
Game Table: Bill and Amy

		Bill's Action		
		Expert Witness	Consultant	Do Nothing
Amy's Action	Discovery	3, 4	5, 7	9, 2
	No Discovery	2, 10	8, 8	12, 4

for this driver is to drive on the left. Hence, an individual driver doesn't have a dominant strategy: the side of the road that's best for this person to drive on depends on which side other drivers choose to drive on.

Even when dominant strategies aren't available and players determine what their best actions are on the basis of what they believe others will choose to do, we can often say something about what might happen. For example, let's assume that all drivers believe that all other drivers will drive on the right. It's rational, then, for Jill to drive on the right. Driving on the right is a rational choice for Jack as well, as it is for every other driver. Hence, we can predict that a status quo in which drivers drive on the right and believe that others will drive on the right will persist: all drivers will continue to believe that all other drivers will drive on the right, and, because of this belief, all drivers will continue to behave exactly as they have been behaving — that is, all will continue to drive on the right.

Such a situation — one in which beliefs and choice of actions reinforce one another and persist — is an *equilibrium*, or a *Nash equilibrium*. That is, a list of named actions (e.g., in the preceding example, each drives on the right), one for each player, is a Nash equilibrium if each player's action is the best one for him, given that he believes the other players will choose their specified actions. In other words, a Nash equilibrium is a situation in which each player answers yes to this question: am I choosing the best action for myself, given what I think others are going to do?

By way of further illustration, let's consider our driving example again, this time assuming that each driver believes that the others will drive on the left. This situation is also a Nash equilibrium: if a driver believes that all other drivers will drive on the left, the driver in question will obviously want to drive on the left as well.

The concept of a Nash equilibrium is a very important one. The main reason is that a Nash equilibrium is a situation that we would naturally say would exist and persist if parties were rational and somehow came to believe that the other parties would choose their Nash equilibrium actions.

Why or exactly how a particular Nash equilibrium arises isn't always immediately obvious, even though such an equilibrium would tend to persist *were* it to arise. If there's more than a single Nash equilibrium, why does one rather than another occur? For instance, why would an equilibrium in which all drivers drive on the right emerge rather than one in which all drivers drive on the left? Why would any equilibrium at all emerge? If some people drive on the left and others drive on the right, why would we expect all people to gravitate to a uniform belief about which side of the road everyone will drive on?

Focal points — beliefs about behaviors that have some kind of psychological salience — provide one possible answer to such questions. For instance, given that people tend to walk on the right, people might think that they would drive on the right as well. In other words, driving on the right might be a focal-point behavior. Another example is this: Two friends are supposed to

---

Box 3
John Nash

The idea of Nash equilibrium was pioneered in the 1950s by John Nash, a mathematician at Princeton. Nash won a Nobel Prize in economics largely for his development of this equilibrium concept. He is the subject of a book and hit movie, *A Beautiful Mind*.

meet at noon in Paris, but they forgot to decide on a specific meeting place. Both might well go to the Eiffel Tower at noon, expecting the other to do the same, given that it's one of the most famous landmarks in the city. In this case, meeting at the Eiffel Tower might be a focal point.

Notions other than focal points sometimes allow players in games to figure out which of several possible Nash equilibrium outcomes is likely to occur. To illustrate, let's consider a variation of the game concerning suit and possible trial that we discussed before. This game is described in Figure 4 (which is the same as Figure 2 except for some of the payoffs).

One Nash equilibrium in this game is for the plaintiff to Lump It and for the defendant to Go to Trial. To see why this is so, suppose that the plaintiff believes that the defendant will Go to Trial. If the plaintiff were to select Sue, she would wind up losing $2,000: she would spend $6,000 on suit and $5,000 more on trial but win only $9,000. (This is the reason for writing −$2,000 at the end of

Figure 4
Litigation Game Tree and the Nash Equilibrium

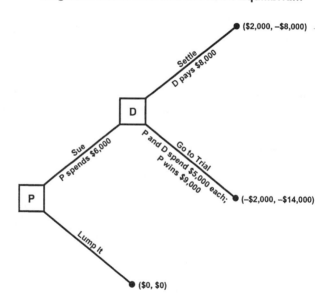

the Go to Trial node.) On the other hand, if the plaintiff chose Lump It, she would end up with nothing, which is better. So the plaintiff will choose Lump It, given her belief that the defendant will choose Go to Trial. Conversely, suppose that the defendant believes that the plaintiff will choose Lump It. The defendant's choice between Settle and Go to Trial doesn't matter — it's irrelevant to him. Thus, for him to choose Go to Trial is a rational option. Hence, we've confirmed that the defendant's choosing Go to Trial and the plaintiff's choosing Lump It constitute a Nash equilibrium.

But there's also a second Nash equilibrium in this example: the plaintiff chooses Sue, and the defendant chooses Settle. To see why, suppose that the plaintiff believes that the defendant will Settle. If the plaintiff chooses Sue, she'll net $2,000: she'll spend $6,000 on suit and receive $8,000 in settlement. If the plaintiff Lumps It, she'll get nothing. So the plaintiff will clearly choose Sue. What about the defendant? If he thinks that the plaintiff will Sue, he's better off choosing Settle and paying $8,000 than he is choosing Go to Trial and winding up losing $14,000. Consequently, it's a Nash equilibrium for the plaintiff to Sue and the defendant to Settle.

Which Nash equilibrium is more plausible? Most of us would say that the second one is. The first equilibrium is unlikely because it's implausible that the defendant would choose Go to Trial. In particular, it would be irrational for the defendant to choose Go to Trial *were* the plaintiff to Sue: if the plaintiff were to Sue, the defendant would then be better off settling for $8,000 than losing $14,000 in trial. This point — that the defendant would not choose Go to Trial — can be expressed in various ways. One way is to say that Go to Trial isn't a *credible* action, isn't a credible threat to the plaintiff, because it wouldn't be carried out if the plaintiff decided to Sue. Another way of putting the point is to say that the only actions that a player ought to believe another player will choose are ones that are rational to choose if and when the choice about the actions actually arises. In the jargon of game

theory, such actions are called *subgame rational* or subgame per-
fect, because they are rational to make in the part of the game
that remains when a choice actually comes up (like the choice
between Settle and Go to Trial for the defendant, once the plaintiff chooses Sue).

You've now been introduced to some of the important concepts
that will enable you to solve games: Sometimes players will have
dominant actions, so they'll choose these actions (as in the prisoners' dilemma game). Sometimes they won't, but there will be a
Nash equilibrium. If there's more than one Nash equilibrium, the
one that will occur will often involve a focal point (e.g., meeting
at the Eiffel Tower) or will involve only actions that are subgame
rational (e.g., ruling out empty threats). These concepts should
help you in thinking about how individuals and firms are likely
to behave in real life. And, as noted earlier, they should also help
you to understand writing that refers to game theory and uses its
vocabulary. We have, of course, merely scratched the surface of a
very large subject. And you might be interested in looking over
the books mentioned at the end of this Handbook and selecting
one to use to pursue game theory further.

Box 4
Can Empty Threats Be Made Credible?

As we discussed, the plaintiff in the litigation game
will think that the defendant won't go to trial and thus
will settle if sued. But the defendant would like to make
the plaintiff believe that he would go to trial. He could
do this by having developed a reputation of going to
trial. Another possibility would be for the defendant to
make some kind of commitment to go to trial (e.g., by
having a lawyer on retainer or a staff of salaried
lawyers in-house).

4. Moral Hazard and Incentives

We're going to switch from game theory to some important topics involving situations in which a party lacks information possessed by another. This subject is relevant to many legal problems; we consider it here because of its particular significance for game theory, though we will note a range of applications. Afterwards, we will turn to a specific game theoretic context in which incomplete information is important, namely, bargaining.

Our first topic on information concerns a phenomenon that got its name from the insurance industry. This industry became aware quite some time ago that ownership of insurance increases the risk that insured parties will incur losses: owning insurance tends to dull the incentive for insured parties to take actions to help prevent losses. For instance, people are naturally less concerned about property losses and thus less careful in preventing fires if they own fire insurance policies than if they don't. The insurance industry dubbed this phenomenon *moral hazard*.

The insurance example of moral hazard typifies an overarching phenomenon: after a contract is made, a party to it may have incentives to act in a way that's detrimental to the other party to the contract. For instance, an employee who's been hired may work less hard than her employer would want. Or a CEO of a

---

Box 5
Moral Hazard and Information

The moral hazard problem is often considered a part of the economics of information. The reason is that the moral hazard problem of undesirable incentives in a contractual relationship is rooted in one party's lack of information about the other party's behavior – such as an insured's fire precautions or an employee's work effort. If the information can be obtained, the problem can be avoided by writing the terms of the contract accordingly.

corporation may make poorer decisions than its shareholders would like. Or a lawyer who has a contract to be paid by the hour may work more hours than his client would wish. Or a recipient of government welfare benefits may not try hard to find a job or to obtain good job training even though the government would want her to.

The moral hazard problem isn't just that having a contract may change the incentives of one party to the disadvantage of the other party. It's that incentives tend to be altered in a way that hurts *both* parties to the contract. To illustrate, let's consider a fire insurance example. Suppose that an insured person can very easily take a precaution — such as closing the fireplace doors when a fire is burning in the fireplace and he's leaving home (closing the doors will prevent embers from escaping into the house and setting it on fire) — and that the cost of the precautionary effort is $10 a year. Suppose, too, that if an insured person takes this precaution, the insurance company would save, on average, $100 a year (according to its actuarial tables). Taking the precaution would be in the mutual interests of the insured individual and the insurer: if the insured would bear the $10 precaution cost, the insurer could afford to reduce the insured's annual insurance premium by more than $10 — say, by $50 — given that the insurer would save $100, so both the insured and the insurer could wind up better off. But, unfortunately, the very fact that the individual is protected by insurance against fire-related losses may lead him not to take the precaution of closing the fireplace doors when he leaves home. Thus, both the insured and the insurer are worse off than they might be.

How can the moral hazard problem be solved? One possibility is for the insurer to *obtain information* about the insured's precautionary behavior. If the insurer can somehow tell whether the insured takes the precaution of closing the fireplace doors, the insurer can induce the insured to do so. For instance, the insurer could lower the annual premium only if the insured closes the fireplace doors, or the insurer could deny coverage for losses if they were caused by failure to close the fireplace doors. More generally, moral hazard problems can be cured if one party to the contract can get information about the possibly problematic behavior or situation of the other party. If an employer can tell how hard an employee is working, the employer can prevent the problem of laxity of effort by rewarding the employee for proper effort or by penalizing the employee for improper effort. If the client who has hired a lawyer on an hourly basis can figure out how many hours the legal task really requires, the client can limit in the contract the number of hours to that number. If the government can find out how hard a welfare recipient searches for a job, it can condition the continuation of benefits on the recipient's exercising proper search effort.

Solving the moral hazard problem with information is one thing. Obtaining the information is another matter. How does an insurer get information about what measures an insured takes to prevent fires? How does an employer obtain information about how hard the employee is working? How do shareholders apprise themselves of the information about business opportunities open to the CEO? How does a client determine how many hours a case ought to take the lawyer?

It depends. Sometimes obtaining information is easy. For instance, it's probably fairly easy for a fire insurer to inspect a person's home to see where smoke detectors are installed. And it's probably not too hard for an employer to find out whether an employee shows up for work and puts in a full day. On the other hand, for an insurance company to determine whether an insured person really closes the fireplace doors when doing so would be appropriate or for an employer to find out whether an employee is taking too many breaks might not be easy. Likewise, ascertaining what business opportunities are available to a CEO or what number of hours is proper for a lawyer to work on a case could be a daunting task.

Difficulty in solving the moral hazard problem through acquisition of information leads to problems for the contracting parties.

Box 6
Insurance Policy Terms and Moral Hazard

Can you explain the following features of insurance policies in view of the moral hazard problem? How do they avoid moral hazard?

- If a worker is disabled, the disability insurance policy will usually limit coverage to, say, 60% of the worker's wage.
- If death is due to suicide, a life insurance policy won't pay benefits.
- If belongings stored in a basement sustain water damage because the basement floods, a homeowner's flood insurance policy won't pay.

One problem is that, although they may solve their problem, they will have to spend money to obtain the information to do so. The insurer may be able to find out whether an insured has installed smoke detectors, but the process of finding out will require paying someone to visit the insured's premises. Another problem is that the acquired information may be fuzzy and imperfect — for example, an employer's information about how hard an employee works or a client's assessment of how many hours a case ought to take may not be very reliable. Therefore, the ability of the employer to motivate the worker properly or the client to set the appropriate number of hours for the lawyer to spend on the case might be poor.

There's a second major way in which moral hazard can be combated: through the use of an *output-based incentive* of some type, such as basing an employee's pay on the employee's contribution to profits. For instance, if the wage of a salesperson in a department store depends on his volume of sales, he'll have a natural incentive to work harder than he would if he were paid only by the hour. If the compensation of a CEO depends significantly on corporate profits, perhaps through stock options, she'll have a motive to choose business opportunities that will increase corporate profits. If an insurance policy doesn't cover losses fully — for example, because it includes a deductible feature or a ceiling on coverage — the insured party will bear part of the loss and will therefore have a reason to reduce the risk of fire. (This is an output-based incentive of a sort, in that the occurrence or nonoccurrence of a fire is an output of whether or not the insured party takes precautionary efforts.)

However, output-based incentives have a big drawback: they impose risk on people. If a CEO's pay is based in substantial part on stock options, her pay will be risky, because the amount will depend on chance elements. If an insured individual is only partially covered against loss, he will, by definition, bear some risk, but risk is exactly what he wants to avoid by purchasing insurance. As a consequence, although output-based incentives can reduce the moral hazard problem, they're often disliked because of risk imposition and are thus of limited utility. More specifically, if too much risk is imposed on a risk-averse contracting party, this party will demand higher compensation (as in the case of a CEO or an employee) or a lower price (as in the case of an insured person), and the cost to the other contracting party may be too high to be worthwhile.

Another difficulty with output-based incentives is that output may be hard to measure. For instance, determining just how much a salesperson contributes to sales may be quite difficult (perhaps one salesperson helps a customer but a different salesperson rings up the sale). Output-based incentives may be hard to fashion in such cases.

In the end, therefore, although moral hazard can be alleviated by two general methods, it typically can't be eliminated. Hence, moral hazard often remains.

A final point is that the existence of moral hazard isn't an argument for government intervention, as is sometimes mistakenly thought to be the case. If workers don't work as hard as would be best or if insured people aren't as careful to prevent loss as would be ideal, this is because the employer or the insurance company is unable to find a worthwhile way to overcome the moral hazard problem by obtaining information or using output-based incentives. Because the government doesn't typically have a superior ability to obtain information or design output-based incentives, there is no call for the government to do anything when moral hazard arises in the private sector.

5. Adverse Selection

Now we're going to turn our sights to another important phenomenon that, like the moral hazard problem, involves asymmetry of information and contracts. It's called *adverse selection*, and it arises in situations in which individuals who differ from each other in important ways selectively choose to enter into contracts.

A famous instance of adverse selection is that of used-car sales and is known as the *lemons problem*. We'd expect to find a larger proportion of cars with problems — so-called lemons — in the used-car market than in the general population of cars. The reason is that people who own lemons would be more likely to try to sell their cars than people whose cars are running well would be. Of course, we wouldn't expect all cars on the used-car market to be lemons. There are, after all, a variety of reasons for wanting to sell perfectly good cars (e.g., the owner might want to buy a new car or might decide to move to a distant city and not drive the car there).

In any case, most prospective used-car buyers will know that used cars carry a relatively high risk of being lemons. Because of this risk, the price that they'll be willing to pay for used cars will tend to be low — that is, lower than it would be if the used-car market included few, if any, lemons. The low price will often be unacceptable to potential sellers of reasonably good used cars, however, and will discourage them from putting their cars up for sale. With fewer cars in decent shape entering the used-car market than would otherwise be the case, the percentage of lemons in the market increases. Hence, the quality problem associated with used cars is exacerbated.

Ultimately, many potential mutually beneficial transactions — between sellers of good used cars and buyers willing to pay an acceptable price for them — will never occur, because the disproportion of lemons lowers the price of used cars. In other words, the tendency for lemons to be selected for sale in the used-car market adversely affects the market in that it prevents the market from functioning in a desirable way.

Adverse selection can be involved in the insurance context as well. Let's consider fire insurance again. We might expect people whose fire risks are relatively high because of the character of their property (e.g., people whose homes don't have good wiring) to be more likely than property owners in general to buy fire insurance. As a consequence, a fire insurer will receive more claims and have to charge higher premiums than it otherwise would. The higher premiums, in turn, will deter some property owners at low risk for fire from buying insurance (or lead them to buy less coverage), even though they'd be willing to pay lower premiums that the insurer would be willing to accept to cover them if it could identify them as the low-risk prospects that they are. In the end, people at high risk for fire tend to buy more insurance coverage. And this adversely affects the functioning of the insurance market by causing premiums to rise and thus leads some people at low risk to buy less coverage than otherwise.

Let's consider one more example: loans, such as bank loans to owners of new restaurants to help them get their restaurants established. We might expect bank loans to be more attractive to owners of restaurants with a lower chance of success than to owners of restaurants with a higher chance of success. The owner of a restaurant that isn't likely to be successful may view a loan as relatively cheap: if the restaurant fails and goes bankrupt, the loan won't have to be repaid. Also, if it's not particularly likely to succeed, its owners (and their friends) might be somewhat reluctant to invest a lot of their own money in the venture. What's the

---

Box 7
Can Warranties Cure Adverse Selection?

In some cases, warranties can be used to avoid the adverse selection problem. For example, a used-car dealer who knows that his cars aren't lemons could guarantee buyers that they aren't — perhaps by agreeing to pay maintenance costs for a year or to take back a car that's frequently in need of repairs. How would this sidestep the adverse selection problem?

---

implication of the tendency for the owners wanting to take out loans to be those whose restaurants are more likely to go bankrupt? It means that the banks will have to charge higher interest rates so as to cover their losses when borrowers go bankrupt. But the higher interest rates discourage borrowing. This also means that owners of some promising new restaurants won't take out loans, even though banks would be willing to lend them money at lower, affordable interest rates if the banks knew these restaurant owners to be unlikely to go bankrupt and thus to be good bets. The problem in the loan market is adverse selection, in which the restaurant owners who take out loans tend to be those who are relatively less likely to repay the loans.

What can be done about adverse selection? One basic response of contracting parties who lack information is to obtain the information they need about their contracting partners. If a prospective buyer of a used car can determine its quality — for instance, by taking it to a service station for inspection — the adverse selection problem will be eliminated: lemons will be recognized as such and sell for low prices, and good used cars will be recognized as well and will sell for appropriately high prices. Therefore, someone contemplating selling a good used car will put the car on the market because he knows that he'll be able to get a fitting price for it, and a buyer who wants such a car, knowing that it isn't a lemon, will willingly pay the fitting price for it. Likewise, in the insurance example, we can imagine that the insurance company will obtain information about the fire risk of prospective policy buyers (e.g., by inspecting their houses to determine the condition of the wiring) and charge those at higher risk more for coverage. Hence, a low-risk buyer wouldn't have to pay a high premium, and the problem of adverse selection would be averted. Note that the adverse selection problem is analogous to the moral hazard problem in that both are due to an asymmetry of information and can be ameliorated in similar ways: by obtaining the appropriate necessary information.

Of course, acquiring information to prevent adverse selection is costly. Some effort is required to have a car inspected to determine whether it's a lemon, and money must be spent to ascertain which risk category a fire insurance purchaser falls into. Hence, information acquisition is, in general, an imperfect remedy for the adverse selection problem. Though it will at times substantially alleviate the problem, often it will not.

One more aspect of the adverse selection problem is that sometimes government action can help to ameliorate it. For example, consider the context of insurance where high-risk individuals cause premiums to go up and the high premiums discourage low-risk individuals from purchasing coverage. In this situation, a rule requiring all individuals to purchase coverage and to pay premiums equal to the average risk might be beneficial, but the details of why are beyond our scope.

6. Bargaining

In ending this Handbook, we're going to take a look at bargaining — something that lawyers do all the time, of course, in making contracts, reaching settlements in litigation, and so forth. For the sake of simplicity, we'll assume that the only issue of concern in bargaining is price. The goal of a party in bargaining is to obtain as large a slice of the available "pie" as possible, but without being so aggressive in making demands that an agreement isn't reached. If either side is too greedy, the deal might fall through, and then no one will be able to enjoy any of the pie. As will become apparent in a moment, this is yet another setting in which asymmetry of information is a crucial issue.

How does a party go about bargaining so as to achieve the goal of obtaining a large slice of the pie without preventing a mutually beneficial deal from being made? One very important factor is a party's *reservation price* — the most that a buyer will pay or the least that a seller will accept. Let's use an example to illustrate the concept of reservation price and why having information about it is valuable.

Suppose that you're selling a piece of land that the prospective buyer would like to build a restaurant on. The buyer's reservation price is the maximum amount that the she'd be willing to pay for the land. This price would be determined by what the restaurant's profits are likely to be, given the location, by how much alternative sites would cost, and so forth. Suppose also that you know the buyer's exact reservation price, that it's $1,000,000. For simplicity, suppose, too, that you can credibly make a single best-and-final demand — a demand that's your only and final one. If you insist on a price that's virtually $1,000,000 — say, $999,000 — you have reason to expect that you'll get this amount.[14] The prospective buyer, truly believing that you'll walk away if she refuses your demand, will rationally accept any price you demand as long as it's less than $1,000,000. You'd thus get the largest possible slice of the contractual pie, and, because your demand wouldn't exceed the buyer's reservation price, you wouldn't prevent the contract for the sale of land from being made.

In practice, of course, you won't know the other side's reservation price. And in trying to get as much as possible, you might end up asking for too much — for an amount that turns out to exceed the buyer's reservation price, which you don't know at the outset — in which case your demand will be rejected. In other words, the more you demand, the better off you'll be *if* a contract

---

14. Can you think of reasons that you might not?

is made but the less likely a contract is to be made. As a result, you'll end up having to make a tradeoff: a higher price will result in a lower likelihood of making the contract. So your best bargaining strategy will usually be one that's less aggressive than it otherwise would be.

This issue is worth considering in greater detail, and we can do this by elaborating on the land-sale example. Suppose again, for simplicity, that you'll make one demand, a take-it-or-leave-it demand that the buyer must either accept or reject. Suppose also that, if you don't sell the land to this buyer, your next-best alternative is to sell to another buyer, one whom you know to be willing to pay $400,000. (That is, your own reservation price is $400,000.)

You must consider what the first potential buyer's reservation price might be. In contrast to the situation we looked at earlier, however, in this case you aren't certain what it is, but suppose that you do know that it is either $700,000 or $1,000,000 (the assumption that it has only two possible values is for convenience only). Suppose, too, that you know that its odds of being $700,000 are 75% and its odds of being $1,000,000 are 25%. If you demand $700,000 (or, rather, slightly below), the buyer will accept regardless of whether her valuation is $700,000 or $1,000,000, and you'll receive $700,000, $300,000 more than the $400,000 from the alternative buyer.

If you demand $1,000,000 (or, rather, slightly below) and the buyer accepts, you'll receive $1,000,000, $600,000 more than from the $400,000 alternative. But the likelihood that this will happen is only 25%. And there's a 75% probability that the buyer's valuation is $700,000, in which case she'll walk away, leaving you with no profit. So, if you ask for $1,000,000, the expected gain over the $400,000 alternative is 25% × $600,000, or $150,000. And this is less than $300,000, the amount you're certain to gain if you ask for $700,000. Hence, you should choose to demand $700,000: demanding $1,000,000 is too aggressive to be in your interest.

Sometimes, however, being tough may make sense for you. In the scenario that we just considered, for example, suppose that there's a 75% chance that the buyer's valuation is the higher amount, $1,000,000. Then insisting on $1,000,000 nets you $600,000 more than the $400,000 alternative 75% of the time. So your expected gain is 75% × $600,000, or $450,000, which is more attractive than the $300,000 gain from the $700,000 demand (unless you're very risk averse).

Having worked through a couple of versions of the land-sale scenario, what generalizations can we make about bargaining strategy?

First, when your bargaining strategy is rational, a mutually beneficial agreement won't necessarily be consummated. The reason is that it may be rational, given your knowledge, to adopt a bargaining stance that's sufficiently tough that, sometimes, the other side will reject it. This was the case in the second version of the land-sale example, the one in which the rational demand was $1,000,000. Demanding this higher amount was rational because the odds were pretty good — 75% — that the buyer placed a high valuation on the land and thus would accept the high demand. But if this turned out to be incorrect and the buyer placed a low valuation on the land, she would reject the demand.

Second, the main lessons that the land-sale scenario drives home are robust: they carry over to more complicated and realistic descriptions of the bargaining process involving, for example, multiple rounds of bargaining. Most bargaining, needless to say, consists of a series of offers and counteroffers. In such settings, as in our land-sale scenario, parties can rationally formulate the demands that they ought to make, given their uncertain knowledge of each other's situation. Sometimes deals will fall through because a party attempted to grab too large a piece of the pie and misgauged the other side's reservation price.

Third, when you're considering how to go about bargaining, you'll most likely find that the kinds of calculations we used in the example will serve you well as a benchmark. This is not to deny that bargaining is, in many respects, an art. Admittedly, there are elements of the other side's psychology that aren't easily assessed or summarized but are important in determining the result that you'll achieve. Nevertheless, you'll find that using calculations of the type illustrated in the example will help you to systematically compare different types of bargaining stances against one another.

7. Suggestions for Further Reading

Many books on game theory have been published. Here are a few recommendations for you to examine if you're interested in exploring the subject further. Thomas Schelling, *The Strategy of Conflict* (Cambridge, Mass.: Harvard University Press, 1960), is a famous early study of game theoretic issues and is written in an informal accessible style. Avinash Dixit and Barry Nalebuff, *Thinking Strategically: The Competitive Edge in Business, Politics, and Everyday Life* (New York: Norton, 1991), is a modern wide-ranging nontechnical book on game theory and is highly readable. A work of special interest for lawyers is Douglas Baird, Robert Gertner, and Randall Picker, *Game Theory and the Law* (Cambridge, Mass.: Harvard University Press, 1994). An easy-to-digest chapter on game theory in a microeconomics textbook is chapter 13 of Robert S. Pindyck and Daniel L. Rubinfeld, *Microeconomics*, 5th ed. (Englewood Cliffs, N.J.: Prentice-Hall, 2001). A more technical but well-exposited book on game theory is Eric Rasmusen, *Games and Information*, 3rd ed. (Malden, Mass.: Blackwell Publishing, Ltd., 2001). An advanced, comprehensive treatment of the subject of game theory is contained in the modern classic, Drew Fudenberg and Jean Tirole, *Game Theory* (Cambridge, Mass.: MIT Press, 1991).

For references on moral hazard, adverse selection, and bargaining, you'll find Baird et al., Rasmusen, as well as chapter 17 of Pindyck and Rubinfeld to be useful.

Appendix

HOMEOWNERS 6
UNIT-OWNERS FORM

AGREEMENT

We will provide the insurance described in this policy in return for the premium and compliance with all applicable provisions of this policy.

DEFINITIONS

In this policy, "you" and "your" refer to the "named insured" shown in the Declarations and the spouse if a resident of the same household. "We," "us" and "our" refer to the Company providing this insurance. In addition, certain words and phrases are defined as follows:

1. "Bodily injury" means bodily harm, sickness or disease, including required care, loss of services and death that results.

2. "Business" includes trade, profession or occupation.

3. "Insured" means you and residents of your household who are:

   a. Your relatives; or

   b. Other persons under the age of 21 and in the care of any person named above.

   Under Section II, "insured" also means:

   c. With respect to animals or watercraft to which this policy applies, any person or organization legally responsible for these animals or watercraft which are owned by you or any person included in 3.a. or 3.b. above. A person or organization using or having custody of these animals or watercraft in the course of any "business" or without consent of the owner is not an "insured";

   d. With respect to any vehicle to which this policy applies:

      (1) Persons while engaged in your employ or that of any person included in 3.a. or 3.b. above; or

      (2) Other persons using the vehicle on an "insured location" with your consent.

4. "Insured location" means:

   a. The "residence premises";

   b. The part of other premises, other structures and grounds used by you as a residence and:

      (1) Which is shown in the Declarations; or

      (2) Which is acquired by you during the policy period for your use as a residence;

   c. Any premises used by you in connection with a premises in 4.a. and 4.b. above;

   d. Any part of a premises:

      (1) Not owned by an "insured"; and

      (2) Where an "insured" is temporarily residing;

   e. Vacant land, other than farm land, owned by or rented to an "insured";

   f. Land owned by or rented to an "insured" on which a one or two family dwelling is being built as a residence for an "insured";

   g. Individual or family cemetery plots or burial vaults of an "insured"; or

   h. Any part of a premises occasionally rented to an "insured" for other than "business" use.

5. "Occurrence" means an accident, including continuous or repeated exposure to substantially the same general harmful conditions, which results, during the policy period, in:

   a. "Bodily injury"; or

   b. "Property damage."

6. "Property damage" means physical injury to, destruction of, or loss of use of tangible property.

7. "Residence employee" means:

   a. An employee of an "insured" whose duties are related to the maintenance or use of the "residence premises," including household or domestic services; or

   b. One who performs similar duties elsewhere not related to the "business" of an "insured."

8. "Residence premises" means the unit where you reside shown as the "residence premises" in the Declarations.

SECTION I — PROPERTY COVERAGES

COVERAGE A — Dwelling

We cover:

1. The alterations, appliances, fixtures and improvements which are part of the building contained within the "residence premises";

2. Items of real property which pertain exclusively to the "residence premises";

3. Property which is your insurance responsibility under a corporation or association of property owners agreement; or

4. Structures owned solely by you, other than the "residence premises," at the location of the "residence premises."

This coverage does not apply to land, including land on which the "residence premises," real property or structures are located.

We do not cover:

1. Structures used in whole or in part for "business" purposes; or

2. Structures rented or held for rental to any person not a tenant of the "residence premises," unless used solely as a private garage.

COVERAGE C — Personal Property

We cover personal property owned or used by an "insured" while it is anywhere in the world. At your request, we will cover personal property owned by:

1. Others while the property is on the part of the "residence premises" occupied by an "insured";

2. A guest or a "residence employee," while the property is in any residence occupied by an "insured."

Our limit of liability for personal property usually located at an "insured's" residence, other than the "residence premises," is 10% of the limit of liability for Coverage C, or $1000, whichever is greater. Personal property in a newly acquired principal residence is not subject to this limitation for the 30 days from the time you begin to move the property there.

Special Limits of Liability. These limits do not increase the Coverage C limit of liability. The special limit for each numbered category below is the total limit for each loss for all property in that category.

1. $200 on money, bank notes, bullion, gold other than goldware, silver other than silverware, platinum, coins and medals.

2. $1000 on securities, accounts, deeds, evidences of debt, letters of credit, notes other than bank notes, manuscripts, personal records, passports, tickets and stamps. This dollar limit applies to these categories regardless of the medium (such as paper or computer software) on which the material exists.

   This limit includes the cost to research, replace or restore the information from the lost or damaged material.

3. $1000 on watercraft, including their trailers, furnishings, equipment and outboard engines or motors.

4. $1000 on trailers not used with watercraft.

5. $1000 for loss by theft of jewelry, watches, furs, precious and semi-precious stones.

6. $2000 for loss by theft of firearms.

7. $2500 for loss by theft of silverware, silver-plated ware, goldware, gold-plated ware and pewterware. This includes flatware, hollowware, tea sets, trays and trophies made of or including silver, gold or pewter.

8. $2500 on property, on the "residence premises," used at any time or in any manner for any "business" purpose.

9. $250 on property, away from the "residence premises," used at any time or in any manner for any "business" purpose. However, this limit does not apply to loss to adaptable electronic apparatus as described in Special Limits **10.** and **11.** below.

10. $1000 for loss to electronic apparatus, while in or upon a motor vehicle or other motorized land conveyance, if the electronic apparatus is equipped to be operated by power from the electrical system of the vehicle or conveyance while retaining its capability of being operated by other sources of power. Electronic apparatus includes:

    a. Accessories or antennas; or

    b. Tapes, wires, records, discs or other media;

    for use with any electronic apparatus.

         HO 00 06 04 91

11. $1000 for loss to electronic apparatus, while not in or upon a motor vehicle or other motorized land conveyance, if the electronic apparatus:

  a. Is equipped to be operated by power from the electrical system of the vehicle or conveyance while retaining its capability of being operated by other sources of power;

  b. Is away from the "residence premises"; and

  c. Is used at any time or in any manner for any "business" purpose.

  Electronic apparatus includes:

  a. Accessories or antennas; or

  b. Tapes, wires, records, discs or other media;

  for use with any electronic apparatus.

Property Not Covered. We do not cover:

1. Articles separately described and specifically insured in this or other insurance;

2. Animals, birds or fish;

3. Motor vehicles or all other motorized land conveyances. This includes:

  a. Their equipment and accessories; or

  b. Electronic apparatus that is designed to be operated solely by use of the power from the electrical system of motor vehicles or all other motorized land conveyances. Electronic apparatus includes:

   (1) Accessories or antennas; or

   (2) Tapes, wires, records, discs or other media;

   for use with any electronic apparatus.

   The exclusion of property described in 3.a. and 3.b. above applies only while the property is in or upon the vehicle or conveyance.

  We do cover vehicles or conveyances not subject to motor vehicle registration which are:

  a. Used to service an "insured's" residence; or

  b. Designed for assisting the handicapped;

4. Aircraft and parts. Aircraft means any contrivance used or designed for flight, except model or hobby aircraft not used or designed to carry people or cargo;

5. Property of roomers, boarders and other tenants, except property of roomers and boarders related to an "insured";

6. Property in an apartment regularly rented or held for rental to others by an "insured";

7. Property rented or held for rental to others off the "residence premises";

8. "Business" data, including such data stored in:

  a. Books of account, drawings or other paper records; or

  b. Electronic data processing tapes, wires, records, discs or other software media.

  However, we do cover the cost of blank recording or storage media, and of pre-recorded computer programs available on the retail market; or

9. Credit cards or fund transfer cards except as provided in Additional Coverages 6.

COVERAGE D – Loss Of Use

The limit of liability for Coverage D is the total limit for all the coverages that follow.

1. If a loss by a Peril Insured Against under this policy to covered property or the building containing the property, makes the "residence premises" not fit to live in, we cover, at your choice, either of the following. However, if the "residence premises" is not your principal place of residence, we will not provide the option under paragraph b. below.

  a. Additional Living Expense, meaning any necessary increase in living expenses incurred by you so that your household can maintain its normal standard of living; or

  b. Fair Rental Value, meaning the fair rental value of that part of the "residence premises" where you reside less any expenses that do not continue while the premises is not fit to live in.

  Payment under **a.** or **b.** will be for the shortest time required to repair or replace the damage or, if you permanently relocate, the shortest time required for your household to settle elsewhere.

2. If a loss covered under this Section makes that part of the "residence premises" rented to others or held for rental by you not fit to live in, we cover the:

  Fair Rental Value, meaning the fair rental value of that part of the "residence premises" rented to others or held for rental by you less any expenses that do not continue while the premises is not fit to live in.

  Payment will be for the shortest time required to repair or replace that part of the premises rented or held for rental.

3. If a civil authority prohibits you from use of the "residence premises" as a result of direct damage to neighboring premises by a Peril Insured Against in this policy, we cover the Additional Living Expense and Fair Rental Value loss as provided under **1.** and **2.** above for no more than two weeks.

The periods of time under **1., 2.** and **3.** above are not limited by expiration of this policy.

We do not cover loss or expense due to cancellation of a lease or agreement.

ADDITIONAL COVERAGES

1. **Debris Removal.** We will pay your reasonable expense for the removal of:

   a. Debris of covered property if a Peril Insured Against that applies to the damaged property causes the loss; or

   b. Ash, dust or particles from a volcanic eruption that has caused direct loss to a building or property contained in a building.

   This expense is included in the limit of liability that applies to the damaged property. If the amount to be paid for the actual damage to the property plus the debris removal expense is more than the limit of liability for the damaged property, an additional 5% of that limit of liability is available for debris removal expense.

   We will also pay your reasonable expense, up to $500, for the removal from the "residence premises" of:

   a. Your tree(s) felled by the peril of Windstorm or Hail;

   b. Your tree(s) felled by the peril of Weight of Ice, Snow or Sleet; or

   c. A neighbor's tree(s) felled by a Peril Insured Against under Coverage C;

   provided the tree(s) damages a covered structure. The $500 limit is the most we will pay in any one loss regardless of the number of fallen trees.

2. **Reasonable Repairs.** In the event that covered property is damaged by an applicable Peril Insured Against, we will pay the reasonable cost incurred by you for necessary measures taken solely to protect against further damage. If the measures taken involve repair to other damaged property, we will pay for those measures only if that property is covered under this policy and the damage to that property is caused by an applicable Peril Insured Against.

This coverage:

   a. Does not increase the limit of liability that applies to the covered property;

   b. Does not relieve you of your duties, in case of a loss to covered property, as set forth in SECTION I – CONDITION **2.d.**

3. **Trees, Shrubs and Other Plants.** We cover trees, shrubs, plants or lawns, on the "residence premises," for loss caused by the following Perils Insured Against: Fire or lightning, Explosion, Riot or civil commotion, Aircraft, Vehicles not owned or operated by a resident of the "residence premises," Vandalism or malicious mischief or Theft.

We will pay up to 10% of the limit of liability that applies to Coverage C for all trees, shrubs, plants or lawns. No more than $500 of this limit will be available for any one tree, shrub or plant. We do not cover property grown for "business" purposes.

This coverage is additional insurance.

4. **Fire Department Service Charge.** We will pay up to $500 for your liability assumed by contract or agreement for fire department charges incurred when the fire department is called to save or protect covered property from a Peril Insured Against. We do not cover fire department service charges if the property is located within the limits of the city, municipality or protection district furnishing the fire department response.

This coverage is additional insurance. No deductible applies to this coverage.

5. **Property Removed.** We insure covered property against direct loss from any cause while being removed from a premises endangered by a Peril Insured Against and for no more than 30 days while removed. This coverage does not change the limit of liability that applies to the property being removed.

6. **Credit Card, Fund Transfer Card, Forgery and Counterfeit Money.**

   We will pay up to $500 for:

   a. The legal obligation of an "insured" to pay because of the theft or unauthorized use of credit cards issued to or registered in an "insured's" name;

   b. Loss resulting from theft or unauthorized use of a fund transfer card used for deposit, withdrawal or transfer of funds, issued to or registered in an "insured's" name;

c. Loss to an "insured" caused by forgery or alteration of any check or negotiable instrument; and

d. Loss to an "insured" through acceptance in good faith of counterfeit United States or Canadian paper currency.

We do not cover use of a credit card or fund transfer card:

a. By a resident of your household;

b. By a person who has been entrusted with either type of card; or

c. If an "insured" has not complied with all terms and conditions under which the cards are issued.

All loss resulting from a series of acts committed by any one person or in which any one person is concerned or implicated is considered to be one loss.

We do not cover loss arising out of "business" use or dishonesty of an "insured."

This coverage is additional insurance. No deductible applies to this coverage.

Defense:

a. We may investigate and settle any claim or suit that we decide is appropriate. Our duty to defend a claim or suit ends when the amount we pay for the loss equals our limit of liability.

b. If a suit is brought against an "insured" for liability under the Credit Card or Fund Transfer Card coverage, we will provide a defense at our expense by counsel of our choice.

c. We have the option to defend at our expense an "insured" or an "insured's" bank against any suit for the enforcement of payment under the Forgery coverage.

7. Loss Assessment. We will pay up to $1000 for your share of loss assessment charged during the policy period against you by a corporation or association of property owners, when the assessment is made as a result of direct loss to the property, owned by all members collectively, caused by a Peril Insured Against under COVERAGE A — DWELLING, other than earthquake or land shock waves or tremors before, during or after a volcanic eruption.

This coverage applies only to loss assessments charged against you as owner or tenant of the "residence premises."

We do not cover loss assessments charged against you or a corporation or association of property owners by any governmental body.

The limit of $1000 is the most we will pay with respect to any one loss, regardless of the number of assessments.

Condition **1.** Policy Period, under SECTIONS I and II CONDITIONS, does not apply to this coverage.

8. Collapse. We insure for direct physical loss to covered property involving collapse of a building or any part of a building caused only by one or more of the following:

a. Perils Insured Against in COVERAGE C — PERSONAL PROPERTY. These perils apply to covered buildings and personal property for loss insured by this additional coverage;

b. Hidden decay;

c. Hidden insect or vermin damage;

d. Weight of contents, equipment, animals or people;

e. Weight of rain which collects on a roof; or

f. Use of defective material or methods in construction, remodeling or renovation if the collapse occurs during the course of the construction, remodeling or renovation.

Loss to an awning, fence, patio, pavement, swimming pool, underground pipe, flue, drain, cesspool, septic tank, foundation, retaining wall, bulkhead, pier, wharf or dock is not included under items **b.**, **c.**, **d.**, **e.**, and **f.** unless the loss is a direct result of the collapse of a building.

Collapse does not include settling, cracking, shrinking, bulging or expansion.

This coverage does not increase the limit of liability applying to the damaged covered property.

9. Glass or Safety Glazing Material

We cover:

a. The breakage of glass or safety glazing material which is part of a building, storm door or storm window, and covered under Coverage A; and

b. Damage to covered property by glass or safety glazing material which is part of a building, storm door or storm window.

This coverage does not include loss on the "residence premises" if the dwelling has been vacant for more than 30 consecutive days immediately before the loss. A dwelling being constructed is not considered vacant.

Loss for damage to glass will be settled on the basis of replacement with safety glazing materials when required by ordinance or law.

This coverage does not increase the limit of liability that applies to the damaged property.

SECTION I — PERILS INSURED AGAINST

We insure for direct physical loss to the property described in Coverages A and C caused by a peril listed below unless the loss is excluded in SECTION I — EXCLUSIONS.

1. Fire or lightning.

2. Windstorm or hail.

This peril does not include loss to the inside of a building or the property contained in a building caused by rain, snow, sleet, sand or dust unless the direct force of wind or hail damages the building causing an opening in a roof or wall and the rain, snow, sleet, sand or dust enters through this opening.

This peril includes loss to watercraft and their trailers, furnishings, equipment, and outboard engines or motors, only while inside a fully enclosed building.

3. Explosion.

4. Riot or civil commotion.

5. Aircraft, including self-propelled missiles and spacecraft.

6. Vehicles.

This peril does not include loss to a fence, driveway or walk caused by a vehicle owned or operated by a resident of the "residence premises."

7. Smoke, meaning sudden and accidental damage from smoke.

This peril does not include loss caused by smoke from agricultural smudging or industrial operations.

8. Vandalism or malicious mischief.

This peril does not include loss to property on the "residence premises" if the dwelling has been vacant for more than 30 consecutive days immediately before the loss. A dwelling being constructed is not considered vacant.

9. Theft, including attempted theft and loss of property from a known place when it is likely that the property has been stolen.

This peril does not include loss caused by theft

a. Committed by an "insured";

b. In or to a dwelling under construction, or of materials and supplies for use in the construction until the dwelling is finished and occupied; or

c. From that part of a "residence premises" rented by an "insured" to other than an "insured."

This peril does not include loss caused by theft that occurs off the "residence premises" of:

a. Property while at any other residence owned by, rented to, or occupied by an "insured," except while an "insured" is temporarily living there. Property of a student who is an "insured" is covered while at a residence away from home if the student has been there at any time during the 45 days immediately before the loss;

b. Watercraft, and their furnishings, equipment and outboard engines or motors; or

c. Trailers and campers.

10. Falling objects.

This peril does not include loss to the inside of a building or property contained in the building unless the roof or an outside wall of the building is first damaged by a falling object. Damage to the falling object itself is not included.

11. Weight of ice, snow or sleet which causes damage to a building or property contained in the building.

This peril does not include loss to an awning, fence, patio, pavement, swimming pool, foundation, retaining wall, bulkhead, pier, wharf, or dock.

12. Accidental discharge or overflow of water or steam from within a plumbing, heating, air conditioning or automatic fire protective sprinkler system or from within a household appliance. We also pay for tearing out and replacing any part of the building which is covered under Coverage A and on the "residence premises," if necessary to repair the system or appliance from which the water or steam escaped.

This peril does not include loss:

a. On the "residence premises," if the dwelling has been vacant for more than 30 consecutive days immediately before the loss. A dwelling being constructed is not considered vacant;

b. To the system or appliance from which the water or steam escaped;

c. Caused by or resulting from freezing except as provided in the peril of freezing below; or

   HO 00 06 04 91

d. On the "residence premises" caused by accidental discharge or overflow which occurs away from the building where the "residence premises" is located.

In this peril, a plumbing system does not include a sump, sump pump or related equipment.

13. **Sudden and accidental tearing apart, cracking, burning or bulging** of a steam or hot water heating system, an air conditioning or automatic fire protective sprinkler system, or an appliance for heating water.

This peril does not include loss caused by or resulting from freezing except as provided in the peril of freezing below.

14. **Freezing** of a plumbing, heating, air conditioning or automatic fire protective sprinkler system or of a household appliance.

This peril does not include loss on the "residence premises" while unoccupied, unless you have used reasonable care to:

a. Maintain heat in the building; or

b. Shut off the water supply and drain the system and appliances of water.

15. **Sudden and accidental damage from artificially generated electrical current.**

This peril does not include loss to a tube, transistor or similar electronic component.

16. **Volcanic eruption** other than loss caused by earthquake, land shock waves or tremors.

SECTION I—EXCLUSIONS

We do not insure for loss caused directly or indirectly by any of the following. Such loss is excluded regardless of any other cause or event contributing concurrently or in any sequence to the loss.

1. **Ordinance or Law,** meaning enforcement of any ordinance or law regulating the construction, repair, or demolition of a building or other structure, unless specifically provided under this policy.

2. **Earth Movement,** meaning earthquake including land shock waves or tremors before, during or after a volcanic eruption; landslide; mine subsidence; mudflow; earth sinking, rising or shifting; unless direct loss by:

   a. Fire;

   b. Explosion; or

   c. Breakage of glass or safety glazing material which is part of a building, storm door or storm window;

   ensues and then we will pay only for the ensuing loss.

   This exclusion does not apply to loss by theft.

3. **Water Damage,** meaning:

   a. Flood, surface water, waves, tidal water, overflow of a body of water, or spray from any of these, whether or not driven by wind;

   b. Water which backs up through sewers or drains or which overflows from a sump; or

   c. Water below the surface of the ground, including water which exerts pressure on or seeps or leaks through a building, sidewalk, driveway, foundation, swimming pool or other structure.

Direct loss by fire, explosion or theft resulting from water damage is covered.

4. **Power Failure,** meaning the failure of power or other utility service if the failure takes place off the "residence premises." But, if a Peril Insured Against ensues on the "residence premises," we will pay only for that ensuing loss.

5. **Neglect,** meaning neglect of the "insured" to use all reasonable means to save and preserve property at and after the time of a loss.

6. **War,** including the following and any consequence of any of the following:

   a. Undeclared war, civil war, insurrection, rebellion or revolution;

   b. Warlike act by a military force or military personnel; or

   c. Destruction, seizure or use for a military purpose.

   Discharge of a nuclear weapon will be deemed a warlike act even if accidental.

7. **Nuclear Hazard,** to the extent set forth in the Nuclear Hazard Clause of SECTION I — CONDITIONS.

8. **Intentional Loss,** meaning any loss arising out of any act committed:

   a. By or at the direction of an "insured"; and

   b. With the intent to cause a loss.

SECTION I — CONDITIONS

1. **Insurable Interest and Limit of Liability.** Even if more than one person has an insurable interest in the property covered, we will not be liable in any one loss:

   a. To the "insured" for more than the amount of the "insured's" interest at the time of loss; or

   b. For more than the applicable limit of liability.

2. **Your Duties After Loss.** In case of a loss to covered property, you must see that the following are done:

   a. Give prompt notice to us or our agent;

   b. Notify the police in case of loss by theft;

   c. Notify the credit card or fund transfer card company in case of loss under Credit Card or Fund Transfer Card coverage;

   d. Protect the property from further damage. If repairs to the property are required, you must

   (1) Make reasonable and necessary repairs to protect the property; and

   (2) Keep an accurate record of repair expenses;

   e. Prepare an inventory of damaged personal property showing the quantity, description, actual cash value and amount of loss. Attach all bills, receipts and related documents that justify the figures in the inventory;

   f. As often as we reasonably require:

   (1) Show the damaged property;

   (2) Provide us with records and documents we request and permit us to make copies; and

   (3) Submit to examination under oath, while not in the presence of any other "insured," and sign the same;

   g. Send to us, within 60 days after our request, your signed, sworn proof of loss which sets forth, to the best of your knowledge and belief:

   (1) The time and cause of loss;

   (2) The interest of the "insured" and all others in the property involved and all liens on the property;

   (3) Other insurance which may cover the loss;

   (4) Changes in title or occupancy of the property during the term of the policy;

   (5) Specifications of damaged buildings and detailed repair estimates;

   (6) The inventory of damaged personal property described in 2.e. above;

   (7) Receipts for additional living expenses incurred and records that support the fair rental value loss; and

   (8) Evidence or affidavit that supports a claim under the Credit Card, Fund Transfer Card, Forgery and Counterfeit Money coverage, stating the amount and cause of loss.

3. **Loss Settlement.** Covered property losses are settled as follows:

   a. Personal property at actual cash value at the time of loss but not more than the amount required to repair or replace.

   b. Coverage A — Dwelling:

   (1) If the damage is repaired or replaced within a reasonable time, at the actual cost to repair or replace;

   (2) If the damage is not repaired or replaced, at actual cash value but not more than the amount required to repair or replace.

4. **Loss to a Pair or Set.** In case of loss to a pair or set we may elect to:

   a. Repair or replace any part to restore the pair or set to its value before the loss; or

   b. Pay the difference between actual cash value of the property before and after the loss.

5. **Glass Replacement.** Loss for damage to glass caused by a Peril Insured Against will be settled on the basis of replacement with safety glazing materials when required by ordinance or law.

6. **Appraisal.** If you and we fail to agree on the amount of loss, either may demand an appraisal of the loss. In this event, each party will choose a competent appraiser within 20 days after receiving a written request from the other. The two appraisers will choose an umpire. If they cannot agree upon an umpire within 15 days, you or we may request that the choice be made by a judge of a court of record in the state where the "residence premises" is located. The appraisers will separately set the amount of loss. If the appraisers submit a written report of an agreement to us, the amount agreed upon will be the amount of loss. If they fail to agree, they will submit their differences to the umpire. A decision agreed to by any two will set the amount of loss.

HO 00 06 04 91

Each party will:

a. Pay its own appraiser; and

b. Bear the other expenses of the appraisal and umpire equally.

7. **Other Insurance.** If a loss covered by this policy is also covered by other insurance, except insurance in the name of a corporation or association of property owners, we will pay only the proportion of the loss that the limit of liability that applies under this policy bears to the total amount of insurance covering the loss.

If, at the time of loss, there is other insurance in the name of a corporation or association of property owners covering the same property covered by this policy, this insurance will be excess over the amount recoverable under such other insurance.

8. **Suit Against Us.** No action can be brought unless the policy provisions have been complied with and the action is started within one year after the date of loss.

9. **Our Option.** If we give you written notice within 30 days after we receive your signed, sworn proof of loss, we may repair or replace any part of the damaged property with like property.

10. **Loss Payment.** We will adjust all losses with you. We will pay you unless some other person is named in the policy or is legally entitled to receive payment. Loss will be payable 60 days after we receive your proof of loss and:

a. Reach an agreement with you;

b. There is an entry of a final judgment; or

c. There is a filing of an appraisal award with us.

11. **Abandonment of Property.** We need not accept any property abandoned by an "insured."

12. **Mortgage Clause.**

The word "mortgagee" includes trustee.

If a mortgagee is named in this policy, any loss payable under Coverage A — Dwelling will be paid to the mortgagee and you, as interests appear. If more than one mortgagee is named, the order of payment will be the same as the order of precedence of the mortgages.

If we deny your claim, that denial will not apply to a valid claim of the mortgagee, if the mortgagee:

a. Notifies us of any change in ownership, occupancy or substantial change in risk of which the mortgagee is aware;

b. Pays any premium due under this policy on demand if you have neglected to pay the premium; and

c. Submits a signed, sworn statement of loss within 60 days after receiving notice from us of your failure to do so. Policy conditions relating to Appraisal, Suit Against Us and Loss Payment apply to the mortgagee.

If we decide to cancel or not to renew this policy, the mortgagee will be notified at least 10 days before the date cancellation or nonrenewal takes effect.

If we pay the mortgagee for any loss and deny payment to you:

a. We are subrogated to all the rights of the mortgagee granted under the mortgage on the property; or

b. At our option, we may pay to the mortgagee the whole principal on the mortgage plus any accrued interest. In this event, we will receive a full assignment and transfer of the mortgage and all securities held as collateral to the mortgage debt.

Subrogation will not impair the right of the mortgagee to recover the full amount of the mortgagee's claim.

13. **No Benefit to Bailee.** We will not recognize any assignment or grant any coverage that benefits a person or organization holding, storing or moving property for a fee regardless of any other provision of this policy.

14. **Nuclear Hazard Clause.**

a. "Nuclear Hazard" means any nuclear reaction, radiation, or radioactive contamination, all whether controlled or uncontrolled or however caused, or any consequence of any of these.

b. Loss caused by the nuclear hazard will not be considered loss caused by fire, explosion, or smoke, whether these perils are specifically named in or otherwise included within the Perils Insured Against in Section I.

c. This policy does not apply under Section I to loss caused directly or indirectly by nuclear hazard, except that direct loss by fire resulting from the nuclear hazard is covered.

15. **Recovered Property.** If you or we recover any property for which we have made payment under this policy, you or we will notify the other of the recovery. At your option, the property will be returned to or retained by you or it will become our property. If the recovered property is returned to or retained by you, the loss payment will be adjusted based on the amount you received for the recovered property.

16. **Volcanic Eruption Period.** One or more volcanic eruptions that occur within a 72-hour period will be considered as one volcanic eruption.

SECTION II – LIABILITY COVERAGES

COVERAGE E – Personal Liability

If a claim is made or a suit is brought against an "insured" for damages because of "bodily injury" or "property damage" caused by an "occurrence" to which this coverage applies, we will:

1. Pay up to our limit of liability for the damages for which the "insured" is legally liable. Damages include prejudgment interest awarded against the "insured"; and

2. Provide a defense at our expense by counsel of our choice, even if the suit is groundless, false or fraudulent. We may investigate and settle any claim or suit that we decide is appropriate. Our duty to settle or defend ends when the amount we pay for damages resulting from the "occurrence" equals our limit of liability.

COVERAGE F – Medical Payments To Others

We will pay the necessary medical expenses that are incurred or medically ascertained within three years from the date of an accident causing "bodily injury." Medical expenses means reasonable charges for medical, surgical, x-ray, dental, ambulance, hospital, professional nursing, prosthetic devices and funeral services. This coverage does not apply to you or regular residents of your household except "residence employees." As to others, this coverage applies only:

1. To a person on the "insured location" with the permission of an "insured"; or

2. To a person off the "insured location," if the "bodily injury":

   a. Arises out of a condition on the "insured location" or the ways immediately adjoining;

   b. Is caused by the activities of an "insured";

   c. Is caused by a "residence employee" in the course of the "residence employee's" employment by an "insured"; or

   d. Is caused by an animal owned by or in the care of an "insured."

SECTION II – EXCLUSIONS

1. **Coverage E – Personal Liability** and **Coverage F – Medical Payments to Others** do not apply to "bodily injury" or "property damage":

   a. Which is expected or intended by the "insured";

   b. Arising out of or in connection with a "business" engaged in by an "insured." This exclusion applies but is not limited to an act or omission, regardless of its nature or circumstance, involving a service or duty rendered, promised, owed, or implied to be provided because of the nature of the "business";

   c. Arising out of the rental or holding for rental of any part of any premises by an "insured." This exclusion does not apply to the rental or holding for rental of an "insured location":

      (1) On an occasional basis if used only as a residence;

      (2) In part for use only as a residence, unless a single family unit is intended for use by the occupying family to lodge more than two roomers or boarders; or

      (3) In part, as an office, school, studio or private garage;

 HO 00 06 04 91

d. Arising out of the rendering of or failure to render professional services;

e. Arising out of a premises:

(1) Owned by an "insured";

(2) Rented to an "insured"; or

(3) Rented to others by an "insured";

that is not an "insured location";

f. Arising out of:

(1) The ownership, maintenance, use, loading or unloading of motor vehicles or all other motorized land conveyances, including trailers, owned or operated by or rented or loaned to an "insured";

(2) The entrustment by an "insured" of a motor vehicle or any other motorized land conveyance to any person; or

(3) Vicarious liability, whether or not statutorily imposed, for the actions of a child or minor using a conveyance excluded in paragraph **(1)** or **(2)** above.

This exclusion does not apply to:

(1) A trailer not towed by or carried on a motorized land conveyance;

(2) A motorized land conveyance designed for recreational use off public roads, not subject to motor vehicle registration and:

(a) Not owned by an "insured"; or

(b) Owned by an "insured" and on an "insured location";

(3) A motorized golf cart when used to play golf on a golf course;

(4) A vehicle or conveyance not subject to motor vehicle registration which is:

(a) Used to service an "insured's" residence;

(b) Designed for assisting the handicapped; or

(c) In dead storage on an "insured location";

g. Arising out of:

(1) The ownership, maintenance, use, loading or unloading of an excluded watercraft described below;

(2) The entrustment by an "insured" of an excluded watercraft described below to any person; or

(3) Vicarious liability, whether or not statutorily imposed, for the actions of a child or minor using an excluded watercraft described below.

Excluded watercraft are those that are principally designed to be propelled by engine power or electric motor, or are sailing vessels, whether owned by or rented to an "insured." This exclusion does not apply to watercraft:

(1) That are not sailing vessels and are powered by:

(a) Inboard or inboard-outdrive engine or motor power of 50 horsepower or less not owned by an "insured";

(b) Inboard or inboard-outdrive engine or motor power of more than 50 horsepower not owned by or rented to an "insured";

(c) One or more outboard engines or motors with 25 total horsepower or less;

(d) One or more outboard engines or motors with more than 25 total horsepower if the outboard engine or motor is not owned by an "insured";

(e) Outboard engines or motors of more than 25 total horsepower owned by an "insured" if:

(i) You acquire them prior to the policy period; and

(a) You declare them at policy inception; or

(b) Your intention to insure is reported to us in writing within 45 days after you acquire the outboard engines or motors.

(ii) You acquire them during the policy period.

This coverage applies for the policy period.

(2) That are sailing vessels, with or without auxiliary power:

(a) Less than 26 feet in overall length;

(b) 26 feet or more in overall length, not owned by or rented to an "insured."

(3) That are stored;

h. Arising out of:

(1) The ownership, maintenance, use, loading or unloading of an aircraft;

(2) The entrustment by an "insured" of an aircraft to any person; or

(3) Vicarious liability, whether or not statutorily imposed, for the actions of a child or minor using an aircraft.

An aircraft means any contrivance used or designed for flight, except model or hobby aircraft not used or designed to carry people or cargo;

i. Caused directly or indirectly by war, including the following and any consequence of any of the following:

(1) Undeclared war, civil war, insurrection, rebellion or revolution;

(2) Warlike act by a military force or military personnel; or

(3) Destruction, seizure or use for a military purpose.

Discharge of a nuclear weapon will be deemed a warlike act even if accidental;

j. Which arises out of the transmission of a communicable disease by an "insured";

k. Arising out of sexual molestation, corporal punishment or physical or mental abuse; or

l. Arising out of the use, sale, manufacture, delivery, transfer or possession by any person of a Controlled Substance(s) as defined by the Federal Food and Drug Law at 21 U.S.C.A. Sections 811 and 812. Controlled Substances include but are not limited to cocaine, LSD, marijuana and all narcotic drugs. However, this exclusion does not apply to the legitimate use of prescription drugs by a person following the orders of a licensed physician.

Exclusions e., f., g., and h. do not apply to "bodily injury" to a "residence employee" arising out of and in the course of the "residence employee's" employment by an "insured".

2. Coverage E — Personal Liability, does not apply to:

a. Liability:

(1) For any loss assessment charged against you as a member of an association, corporation or community of property owners;

(2) Under any contract or agreement. However, this exclusion does not apply to written contracts:

(a) That directly relate to the ownership, maintenance or use of an "insured location"; or

(b) Where the liability of others is assumed by the "insured" prior to an "occurrence";

unless excluded in (1) above or elsewhere in this policy;

b. "Property damage" to property owned by the "insured";

c. "Property damage" to property rented to, occupied or used by or in the care of the "insured." This exclusion does not apply to "property damage" caused by fire, smoke or explosion;

d. "Bodily injury" to any person eligible to receive any benefits:

(1) Voluntarily provided; or

(2) Required to be provided;

by the "insured" under any:

(1) Workers' compensation law;

(2) Non-occupational disability law; or

(3) Occupational disease law;

e. "Bodily injury" or "property damage" for which an "insured" under this policy:

(1) Is also an insured under a nuclear energy liability policy; or

(2) Would be an insured under that policy but for the exhaustion of its limit of liability.

A nuclear energy liability policy is one issued by:

(1) American Nuclear Insurers;

(2) Mutual Atomic Energy Liability Underwriters;

(3) Nuclear Insurance Association of Canada;

or any of their successors; or

f. "Bodily injury" to you or an "insured" within the meaning of part a. or b. of "insured" as defined.

3. Coverage F — Medical Payments to Others, does not apply to "bodily injury":

a. To a "residence employee" if the "bodily injury":

(1) Occurs off the "insured location"; and

(2) Does not arise out of or in the course of the "residence employee's" employment by an "insured";

b. To any person eligible to receive benefits:

(1) Voluntarily provided; or

(2) Required to be provided;

under any:

(1) Workers' compensation law;

(2) Non-occupational disability law; or

(3) Occupational disease law;

                   HO 00 06 04 91

c. From any:

(1) Nuclear reaction;

(2) Nuclear radiation; or

(3) Radioactive contamination;

all whether controlled or uncontrolled or how-ever caused; or

(4) Any consequence of any of these; or

d. To any person, other than a "residence em-ployee" of an "insured," regularly residing on any part of the "insured location."

SECTION II – ADDITIONAL COVERAGES

We cover the following in addition to the limits of liabil-ity:

1. Claim Expenses. We pay:

   a. Expenses we incur and costs taxed against an "insured" in any suit we defend;

   b. Premiums on bonds required in a suit we de-fend, but not for bond amounts more than the limit of liability for Coverage E. We need not apply for or furnish any bond;

   c. Reasonable expenses incurred by an "insured" at our request, including actual loss of earnings (but not loss of other income) up to $50 per day, for assisting us in the investigation or de-fense of a claim or suit; and

   d. Interest on the entire judgment which accrues after entry of the judgment and before we pay or tender, or deposit in court that part of the judgment which does not exceed the limit of li-ability that applies.

2. First Aid Expenses. We will pay expenses for first aid to others incurred by an "insured" for "bodily in-jury" covered under this policy. We will not pay for first aid to you or any other "insured."

3. Damage to Property of Others. We will pay, at replacement cost, up to $500 per "occurrence" for "property damage" to property of others caused by an "insured."

   We will not pay for "property damage":

   a. To the extent of any amount recoverable under Section I of this policy;

   b. Caused intentionally by an "insured" who is 13 years of age or older;

   c. To property owned by an "insured";

   d. To property owned by or rented to a tenant of an "insured" or a resident in your household; or

   e. Arising out of:

      (1) A "business" engaged in by an "insured";

      (2) Any act or omission in connection with a premises owned, rented or controlled by an "insured," other than the "insured location"; or

(3) The ownership, maintenance, or use of aircraft, watercraft or motor vehicles or all other motorized land conveyances.

This exclusion does not apply to a motor-ized land conveyance designed for recrea-tional use off public roads, not subject to motor vehicle registration and not owned by an "insured."

4. Loss Assessment. We will pay up to $1000 for your share of loss assessment charged during the policy period against you by a corporation or asso-ciation of property owners, when the assessment is made as a result of:

   a. "Bodily injury" or "property damage" not ex-cluded under Section II of this policy; or

   b. Liability for an act of a director, officer or trus-tee in the capacity as a director, officer or trus-tee; provided:

      (1) The director, officer or trustee is elected by the members of a corporation or association of property owners; and

      (2) The director, officer or trustee serves with-out deriving any income from the exercise of duties which are solely on behalf of a corporation or association of property own-ers.

This coverage applies only to loss assessments charged against you as owner or tenant of the "residence premises."

We do not cover loss assessments charged against you or a corporation or association of property owners by any governmental body.

Regardless of the number of assessments, the limit of $1000 is the most we will pay for loss aris-ing out of:

   a. One accident, including continuous or repeated exposure to substantially the same general harmful condition; or

b. A covered act of a director, officer or trustee. An act involving more than one director, officer or trustee is considered to be a single act.

The following do not apply to this coverage:

1. Section II – Coverage E – Personal Liability Exclusion 2.a.(1);
2. Condition 1. Policy Period, under SECTIONS I AND II CONDITIONS.

SECTION II – CONDITIONS

1. **Limit of Liability.** Our total liability under Coverage E for all damages resulting from any one "occurrence" will not be more than the limit of liability for Coverage E as shown in the Declarations. This limit is the same regardless of the number of "insureds," claims made or persons injured. All "bodily injury" and "property damage" resulting from any one accident or from continuous or repeated exposure to substantially the same general harmful conditions shall be considered to be the result of one "occurrence."

   Our total liability under Coverage F for all medical expense payable for "bodily injury" to one person as the result of one accident will not be more than the limit of liability for Coverage F as shown in the Declarations.

2. **Severability of Insurance.** This insurance applies separately to each "insured." This condition will not increase our limit of liability for any one "occurrence."

3. **Duties After Loss.** In case of an accident or "occurrence," the "insured" will perform the following duties that apply. You will help us by seeing that these duties are performed:

   a. Give written notice to us or our agent as soon as is practical, which sets forth:

      (1) The identity of the policy and "insured";
      (2) Reasonably available information on the time, place and circumstances of the accident or "occurrence"; and
      (3) Names and addresses of any claimants and witnesses;

   b. Promptly forward to us every notice, demand, summons or other process relating to the accident or "occurrence";

   c. At our request, help us:

      (1) To make settlement;
      (2) To enforce any right of contribution or indemnity against any person or organization who may be liable to an "insured";
      (3) With the conduct of suits and attend hearings and trials; and
      (4) To secure and give evidence and obtain the attendance of witnesses;

   d. Under the coverage – Damage to Property of Others – submit to us within 60 days after the loss, a sworn statement of loss and show the damaged property, if in the "insureds" control;

   e. The "insured" will not, except at the "insured's" own cost, voluntarily make payment, assume obligation or incur expense other than for first aid to others at the time of the "bodily injury."

4. **Duties of an Injured Person – Coverage F – Medical Payments to Others.**
   The injured person or someone acting for the injured person will:

   a. Give us written proof of claim, under oath if required, as soon as is practical; and
   b. Authorize us to obtain copies of medical reports and records.

   The injured person will submit to a physical exam by a doctor of our choice when and as often as we reasonably require.

5. **Payment of Claim – Coverage F – Medical Payments to Others.** Payment under this coverage is not an admission of liability by an "insured" or us.

6. **Suit Against Us.** No action can be brought against us unless there has been compliance with the policy provisions.

   No one will have the right to join us as a party to any action against an "insured." Also, no action with respect to Coverage E can be brought against us until the obligation of the "insured" has been determined by final judgment or agreement signed by us.

7. **Bankruptcy of an Insured.** Bankruptcy or insolvency of an "insured" will not relieve us of our obligations under this policy.

8. **Other Insurance – Coverage E – Personal Liability.** This insurance is excess over other valid and collectible insurance except insurance written specifically to cover as excess over the limits of liability that apply in this policy.

 HO 00 06 04 91

SECTIONS I AND II – CONDITIONS

1. **Policy Period.** This policy applies only to loss in Section I or "bodily injury" or "property damage" in Section II, which occurs during the policy period.

2. **Concealment or Fraud.** The entire policy will be void if, whether before or after a loss, an "insured" has:

   a. Intentionally concealed or misrepresented any material fact or circumstance;

   b. Engaged in fraudulent conduct; or

   c. Made false statements;

   relating to this insurance.

3. **Liberalization Clause.** If we make a change which broadens coverage under this edition of our policy without additional premium charge, that change will automatically apply to your insurance as of the date we implement the change in your state, provided that this implementation date falls within 60 days prior to or during the policy period stated in the Declarations.

   This Liberalization Clause does not apply to changes implemented through introduction of a subsequent edition of our policy.

4. **Waiver or Change of Policy Provisions.**

   A waiver or change of a provision of this policy must be in writing by us to be valid. Our request for an appraisal or examination will not waive any of our rights.

5. **Cancellation.**

   a. You may cancel this policy at any time by returning it to us or by letting us know in writing of the date cancellation is to take effect.

   b. We may cancel this policy only for the reasons stated below by letting you know in writing of the date cancellation takes effect. This cancellation notice may be delivered to you, or mailed to you at your mailing address shown in the Declarations.

   Proof of mailing will be sufficient proof of notice.

   (1) When you have not paid the premium, we may cancel at any time by letting you know at least 10 days before the date cancellation takes effect.

   (2) When this policy has been in effect for less than 60 days and is not a renewal with us, we may cancel for any reason by letting you know at least 10 days before the date cancellation takes effect.

   (3) When this policy has been in effect for 60 days or more, or at any time if it is a renewal with us, we may cancel:

      (a) If there has been a material misrepresentation of fact which if known to us would have caused us not to issue the policy; or

      (b) If the risk has changed substantially since the policy was issued.

      This can be done by letting you know at least 30 days before the date cancellation takes effect.

   (4) When this policy is written for a period of more than one year, we may cancel for any reason at anniversary by letting you know at least 30 days before the date cancellation takes effect.

   c. When this policy is cancelled, the premium for the period from the date of cancellation to the expiration date will be refunded pro rata.

   d. If the return premium is not refunded with the notice of cancellation or when this policy is returned to us, we will refund it within a reasonable time after the date cancellation takes effect.

6. **Nonrenewal.** We may elect not to renew this policy. We may do so by delivering to you, or mailing to you at your mailing address shown in the Declarations, written notice at least 30 days before the expiration date of this policy. Proof of mailing will be sufficient proof of notice.

7. **Assignment.** Assignment of this policy will not be valid unless we give our written consent.

8. **Subrogation.** An "insured" may waive in writing before a loss all rights of recovery against any person. If not waived, we may require an assignment of rights of recovery for a loss to the extent that payment is made by us.

   If an assignment is sought, an "insured" must sign and deliver all related papers and cooperate with us.

   Subrogation does not apply under Section II to Medical Payments to Others or Damage to Property of Others.

9. **Death.** If any person named in the Declarations or the spouse, if a resident of the same household, dies:

   a. We insure the legal representative of the deceased but only with respect to the premises and property of the deceased covered under the policy at the time of death;

b. "Insured" includes:

   (1) Any member of your household who is an "insured" at the time of your death, but only while a resident of the "residence premises"; and

(2) With respect to your property, the person having proper temporary custody of the property until appointment and qualification of a legal representative.

Index